On December 14, 2012, an angry young man shot his way through the glass doors of Sandy Hook Elementary School and proceeded to mercilessly gun down twenty first-graders and six teachers and administrators. My 6-year-old son, Jesse, was among those killed. In the midst of my shock and despair, I asked myself the same question the rest of the world was asking: "How could something like this happen?"

I came to the conclusion that an angry thought in the shooter's head was the root cause of the whole tragedy. I pictured the shooter as a young boy, experiencing anger without the tools and nurturing environment to help him process that emotion. Anger is usually the result of pain (whether physical or emotional), and the boy, in his desperation to find relief from these difficult feelings, blamed someone else – as we human beings often do – thinking this would alleviate his pain. In holding someone else responsible for his pain, he gave away all his personal power to change his situation – in essence, becoming a victim. Prolonged feelings of victimization can lead to rage, and I believe rage is what fills our prison systems and leads to acts of violence such as Sandy Hook, as well as the other acts of violence we hear about on the news every night.

The next question I asked myself was, "What can we do to help people with their angry thoughts so that something like this never happens again?" I believe that, on an individual basis, being aware of the nature of our thoughts is the first step. Every person has an average of 60,000 thoughts per day. When you take time to reflect on what you really think about, you may realize (as I did) that perhaps many of these thoughts are not positive, possibly even angry, and that does not serve you. When we become mindful of this, we can, as individuals, work toward replacing these negative thoughts with loving and productive ones.

But how can we help diminish the anger in society as a whole, when our culture is inundated with negative influences like violent video games and movies, broken homes, drugs, and a plethora of other modern stresses that add to our collective fury? I believe the answer is to bring the teaching of values back into our school systems, and our society as a whole. Some people equate values with religion, but as Milan points out, these are not the same. There is no religion that owns ideals such as compassion. Love, truth, peace, right conduct and nonviolence are the values Milan focuses on in this book, and I firmly believe that through embracing these values ourselves and then teaching others to do so, we can create a more peaceful world.

The teaching of values begins in the home, but we cannot take for granted that every child is being exposed to a healthy and nurturing environment. Even in homes where parents have strong values, the hectic nature of daily life can sometimes interfere with our good intentions to discuss the importance of values with our children. While I like to believe that I led by example in my household, I was also a single mother with a full-time job raising two young boys with little help. I don't remember a specific time where I sat my boys down and talked to them directly and purposefully about values.

Curriculum in our modern educational system has been focused on reading, writing and arithmetic, as well as the administering of standardized testing to ensure children are grasping these fundamentals. I believe that in addition to teaching these important skills, we must also impart to our youth a consistent message of values, not only in schools but in our larger communities. We must incorporate these values as guiding principles in all of our public institutions – including hospitals, police departments, government agencies – as well as in our homes. I know this is possible, as I have seen it occurring all over the United States – concerned citizens like you and me are making it happen.

I learned firsthand that the absence of values leads to pain and suffering. Sometimes this anguish can motivate people to grow and become positive influences in society. After our tragedy, JT, my (then) 12-year-old son, and I chose to forgive the man who murdered Jesse. We made a conscious choice to embrace these values and have dedicated our lives to helping others understand the power and potential of choosing love over anger. However, as JT so eloquently stated during an interview, "You don't have to go through a tragedy to grow. You can choose to do it now."

If I could boil my whole experience down to one word, it would be 'choice.' You can't always choose what happens to you, but you can always choose how you respond. Reflection on Milan's five core values allows you to see a difficult situation as an opportunity to grow instead of just another hurdle in your path. With this perspective you can start a trajectory toward peace and joy that is unstoppable, regardless of what comes your way.

I believe this book should be required reading for everyone. Those who already adhere to the five values will find their resolve strengthened, as I have. Those who have not yet embraced these values will be inspired to begin a new life of hope and promise. Sharing these values with our children will help to create a new generation full of optimism and resilience, capable of meeting challenges and adversity with positivity and purpose, not anger and violence.

I know that for me, it is the five values Milan explains in this book, along with gratitude, forgiveness and compassion (love in action), that have allowed me to move forward even during my darkest moments after losing my precious young son. It is these same values that have allowed my surviving son to continue his life with faith and confidence. Indeed, it is choosing to live life guided by the five values that cultivates the courage we all need to go through life productively as grateful, happy and peaceful participants.

—Scarlett Lewis

To support this beautiful message contact:
http://www.jesselewischooselove.org/

back TO THE basics

back TO THE basics

five core values revitalized

Milan Hollister Ph.D.

TATE PUBLISHING
AND ENTERPRISES, LLC

Published by Tate Publishing & Enterprises, LLC
127 E. Trade Center Terrace | Mustang, Oklahoma 73064 USA
1.888.361.9473 | www.tatepublishing.com

Tate Publishing is committed to excellence in the publishing industry. The company reflects the philosophy established by the founders, based on Psalm 68:11,
"The Lord gave the word and great was the company of those who published it."

Cover design by Harold Jason Branzuela
Interior design by Manolito Bastasa

Published in the United States of America

ISBN: 978-1-63185-332-6
1. Body, Mind & Spirit / Inspiration & Personal Growth
14.04.04

To Rick,

for teaching me through patience and understanding

To Annie and Susan,

for always being there for me with love

To my dogs

Meg, Belleza, Lia,

Wiggles (May 1999-January 2014)

who remind me how to live every

moment in the present with love

To S.B.

for opening my heart and changing my life forever

Contents

Prologue

"Character, above all, is the quality that has to be safeguarded by one and all. This alone is God's desire forever...

All are one, be alike to everyone. The entire humanity of the world is a single family. Whether you are an atheist or a theist, youth or aged, you should recognize that you all are part of the single human race. You have to develop human values. Without this, you are human merely in form not fact.

Man is filled with qualities such as anger, greed, desire, and jealousy. These are animal qualities. Many animal qualities are rampant in human beings today. This situation must be corrected." We must go back to the basics and revitalize five core human values.

What are human values? Love, truth, peace, right conduct, and nonviolence.

—Sathya Sai Speaks, Volume–33

The Road Home

> Grief is a great friend, for it opens one's eyes and shocks them to search the secret of peace and happiness.
>
> —Sathya Sai Baba (Indian guru, spiritual figure, and educator)

Silly Metaphors

Life is made up of a lot of silly metaphors. Some of them seem to make a great deal of sense, and other times, they seem to be just auditory annoyances people use in an effort to distract you from the issues at hand. Through my personal trials and tribulations, I have heard more than my fair share. But there always seemed to be one saying that kept coming to the forefront in my life. What people kept reciting seemed to be some sort of standard mantra that was delivered ceremoniously in response to my life turning into and just plain feeling like, shall we say, poo.

For the most part, I have been aware that most people were well-intentioned when they were trying to soothe me with comforting verses, clichés, and metaphors. But I can tell you that at no point during any of my earlier personal disasters did a collective of "helpful" words make me feel any better about myself or situation. In fact, the more people tried to add their two cents, the more it annoyed me as I felt that people didn't really want to understand how bad my life was. There was no catchy phrase that was going to get me out of my pain. I mean, how hard was it for people to comprehend that I was the victim in all this mess called my life? It was certainly crystal clear to me. (At least that was the lie I kept telling myself.) Fast-forward many, many years, and the mantra that everyone kept reciting has come to mean something different from its first introduction. So what was it?

"If you aren't struggling or experiencing some sort of pain, you aren't growing."

My initial thought when I first heard this theory was to ask if there is anything that I could do to "stunt my growth." I figured life was hard enough. Only in a twisted reality would my life have to be crappy for me to experience some sort of positive life "growth spurt." The idea made perfect sense—not. No matter. I was handling things (albeit poorly), and I certainly didn't need some stupid, (seemingly) irrational spiritual logic to try and make me feel better about all the drama going on around me. The idea was incredibly rudimentary and certainly couldn't justify all that was happening to me. Besides, in my mind, my problems were huge—far bigger than any anyone could define with simple reasoning. Moreover, I was certainly not inclined to buy into the notion that I had to be miserable to be "spiritually evolved" or a smarter person. Besides, ignoring my problems and wallowing in my drama felt good (or so I thought). It made me feel significant. I was somebody who had been hurt and damaged by life. I had a reason to be bitter, angry, and unmotivated. My story was a way for me to define who I was and make excuses for living a mediocre life. Moreover, who would I be without my past? Unconsciously, I thought I needed my pain as a shield that protected me from life. However, it only held me back from really feeling, living, or loving. Interestingly, at the same time, it kept me wondering. So as it is, like most people on the planet living with a myriad of lame excuses and outdated stories, I have had ample opportunity in the "school of hard knocks" to try to figure out what those words really meant. But more than that, I had to figure out if I wanted to continue my personal drama or create an entirely different ending for myself.

> I know God will not give me anything I cannot handle. I just wish he didn't trust me so much.
>
> —(Mother Teresa, Catholic nun, humanitarian)

When All Else Fails, Run from Your Problems

My childhood was incredibly tumultuous. Without question, it set me up for the greatest lessons I would learn throughout my life. And although it was a brief introduction into the values, I don't see it as the primary catalyst into my self-exploration. I see it as a time where I was simply surviving from one day to the next. It was a time where I was questioning and hated the *God* that I had come to know. So although the pain of my youth led me to inquiry, it wasn't the final straw that drove me to want to make lasting, positive changes. As such, I need to fast-forward to my late 20s.

In 1999, after I graduated with my bachelor's in psychology, I headed west to pursue a Psy D degree to become a psychologist. As most things in my life, the universe decided to quickly redirect my focus, and at the last minute, I opted to change my major and become a social worker. It seemed more practical, and in truth, the school seemed like it would be a lot more fun. Thirty-three credits into that degree, I realized I had a low tolerance for bureaucracy and a high tolerance for making poor choices. It wasn't a good combination. So I made the decision to get a Master's in Education Counseling and change universities. Truthfully, the degree didn't really make any sense for any of the objectives that I had set for myself. Be that as it may, I moved forward because figuring out what I really wanted seemed far more difficult than going to school for another year and settling for a degree that would never really serve me with much use.

Since school wasn't lighting the fire of passion within me, my need to contribute (or save others) took a front seat in my focus. As such, toward the end of my master's degree, I decided to start a business with the intention that I could do something good for less fortunate children. I had lofty goals of starting a transitional living facility where children could live while they were being placed in more permanent homes and engage in all kinds of wonderful alternative therapies such as art, equestrian, music, etc. I wanted children to be able to live out their dreams and not be limited by their dysfunctional or financially constrained surroundings. I had a million ideas about how to help. At the time, I could not see what my unconscious intentions were in all of my plans. But the reality was that I was really just trying to rescue myself. I was doing for others what I hoped someone would do for me. I wanted to be seen as more than I was and have someone believe that I could do and be anything. However, doing so under the guise of helping others seemed a whole lot nobler.

I worked tirelessly, going to school and building the business. But after six months, I realized the vision of helping the children just wasn't in the cards for me. Since I was trying to save the children because I could not save myself, my objectives and my energy were in conflict with each other. As a result, I could not seem to solicit enough money to keep things going. So I opted to close the door to my dream and move on to whatever life had in store for me. But I felt like a colossal failure. For me, it wasn't just about giving up on the children; I gave up on myself.

> Fate is like a strange, unpopular restaurant filled with odd little waiters who bring you things you never asked for and don't always like.
> —(Lemony Snicket, American novelist)

As fate would have it, right before I closed up shop forever, a group of investment-type people that I had met some months earlier came to me with a proposition that would save the business. However, I was torn as I was already resigned to moving forward in a new direction. At the same time, how could I pass up free money to help those less fortunate? Moreover, I could redeem myself as "the great disappointment." I was conflicted. My inner knowing was telling me to leave things alone and move on. But I went against my intuition (which was screaming no) and agreed to work with the company. That one decision changed my life forever.

> In modern business it is not the crook who is to be feared most, it is the honest man who doesn't know what he is doing.
> —(Pablo Casals, Catalan cellist and conductor)

In 2002, I found out that the men I was working with were well-credentialed crooks, and I was at the hub of their scheme. I was crushed. I had trusted these people to direct my goals and my future. I put so much faith in them, I lost track of my own inner guidance. As a result, I lost everything. I lost my house, my business, money, a fiancé, self-respect, and dignity. At the time, if you would have asked me, to say that I had failed, in fact, would have been an enormous understatement. It was a life-altering experience that led to legal implications and having to take responsibility for the damage done. To this day, the depth of the repercussions and how people were impacted are still beyond my comprehension. And although on a conscious level I may have been clueless as to what was happening with these men, I always had a gut feeling that something was amiss. I just simply chose to ignore the constant nagging because my ego and drive to be significant and to *make* something happen far outweighed (what I perceived to be) my original objective: to do good for the less fortunate. At some point, I had decided not to stick to my value structure. I decided that proving to all the naysayers that I was competent and capable was far more important that my inner knowing.

> Trust is like a vase…once it's broken, though you can fix it the vase will never be the same again.
>
> —(Anonymous)

For about a year after everything was exposed, I lived in constant mind-numbing fear. Nothing that happened during that time of my life produced any kind of warm, fuzzy feeling that made sunshine, smiles, and rainbows. In fact, it was the kind of situation that guts your soul and makes you wish that you never woke up from what you could only hope was a bad dream. It was the sort of problem that takes your breath away and destroys whatever is left of your dignity and self-worth. It was an experience that took whatever was left of my trust in humanity (and myself) and shredded it into a million little bits of confetti-size pieces. My world had become like a perpetually shaken snow globe. I felt trapped in a glass bubble of circumstances. What was left of who I was were the white snowflakes swirling around in a wispy illusion. Anything that was to settle were merely pieces of something that I felt could never be made whole again. I had reached my bottom, which seemed like a hole that extended to the center of the earth's core. I saw no viable way out. I felt like I had nothing left, and my life would never be the same. Little did I know, this was all a blessing hidden in a rather ugly disguise.

> I promise you running away, moving away, will NOT heal what hurts! It just puts a band-aid on a gaping wound. Denial is dangerous!
>
> —(Unknown)

In my first attempt to eradicate myself from the situation, I moved back east. In the middle of my personal storm, an old boyfriend proposed to me. It should have been a happy occasion. However, in my heart, I knew he wasn't the one. But I felt frantic whirling around in the unknown. Subsequently, he was merely a life preserver that I tried to desperately cling to during my personal tsunami. As I quickly found out, it is really hard to be in a relationship with someone who is perpetually suicidal as well as emotionally and financially depleted. That someone was me. I was barely holding myself together. I didn't like or trust anyone, including myself. And I certainly did not feel worthy of happiness. So after a lengthy conversation with him telling me about how I was negatively impacting his finances and causing him stress, I could do nothing for him but take off my engagement ring and suggest that he return it. I had nothing left to give anyone. At that point, the ring was nothing more than a reminder of my unworthiness. Within fifteen minutes of the conversation, he left for the jewelry store with the ring in his hand. Technicially, we were still engaged, but I knew in that moment that it was over. His actions only seemed to reinforce the feelings that I was useless and unlovable. I knew it, but the way he handled things only substantiated it. It was another devastating blow to my already-fragile state.

In response to my world crumbling down around me, I did what any self-respecting coward would do—I decided to run from my problems. I devised a plan to stay with my fiancé long enough to save up about $4,000. Then I bought a one-way ticket to Madrid, Spain, broke it off with my fiancé, left my job, and made arrangements with a friend to leave my dogs. My plan was to go away and never look back. I didn't care about anything but my escape. I figured the farther I was from my problems, the less impact they would have on my life. At the time, the whole idea seemed completely rational to me. Moving and running was already an established pattern in my life. In fact, I was rather skilled at it. So in my thinking, clearly, another continent seemed like an appropriate amount of distance from my troubles. I believed that it would be easy to disappear in a foreign country. I was on a one woman quest to become invisible. It seemed like the only answer to heal my pain. But I never made it to Spain that year.

> Stop running away from your problems because that only increases the distance from the solution. Make it right today, tomorrow is too late.
>
> —(Anonymous)

The last step to eradicating the parts of my existence were to drop my dogs off with my friend. Nothing meant anything to me anymore even my most precious companions. However, I never left the dogs, and I never made it to the airport that year. In fact, I ended up in a tiny remote town in northern Missouri where I spent the next two years working on a journey toward healing. I lived in a log cabin on seven acres surrounded by dozens of walnut trees with a little creek running through the backwoods. I shared that home with my friend who became a significant mother figure and spiritual mentor. She knew that I was broken and my heart and trust shattered. So she opened up her heart and home. She offered me a place to begin my journey back to the basics and reclaim a sense of self.

During those two years, she introduced me to books, a guru, and gave me the support, unconditional love, and comfort that I was so desperately craving. She helped me begin to trust again and mend a broken heart. In the course of that time, I also lived in relative solitude while working through an enormous amount of pain, hurt, and self-loathing. It was exactly what I needed to begin a long-overdue healing process—not just from the business debacle, but from my first thirty-three years of life.

> Sometimes it is the person closest to us who must travel the furthest distance to be our friend."
>
> —(Robert Brault, American operatic tenor)

Those two years in what I fondly dubbed the Park, I learned about relationships—the most important relationship, the connection between myself and God. I came to understand that even though I had been searching for a higher power or some universal answer, my anger toward the concept of God had closed my heart to any possibilities to let Him in. It was the ultimate paradox. I wanted to know and love God but held on to an enormous amount of resentment toward Him for allowing pain and unhappiness into my life. I felt He had continued to abandon me in my times of need. As such, I shut God out. Plus, I certainly had experienced so much rejection in my life. I didn't need to add "God" to what seemed to be a growing list of people who didn't accept or want me. But at the same time, my soul was seeking refuge in the divine as it knew more about the cosmos than my brain could even begin to process. Reflecting back, I now know it was being of my journey toward the five human values.

> Creativity requires the courage to let go of certainties.
>
> —(Erich Fromm, German social psychologist)

During the time of what I dubbed my "radical sabbatical," in addition to my spiritual quest, I also learned a lot of other things about myself. I started to realize that people could (and would) accept and love me for who I was. I also found out that I was creative, not in a van Gogh kind of way, but just enough to be interesting. I also learned that I was very industrious. In those two years in the Park, I learned to crochet, build furniture, chink a log cabin, pick and process walnuts, use a chain saw, drive an industrial lawn mower, and tile a floor (to name just a few things). Although not exactly in the scope of artistic, I also learned how to pluck my eyebrows and use night cream.

For those two years, I am sure my friends and family were convinced that I was living in some sort of institution where I was only allowed to send gifts from my arts and crafts class. At one point, I made everyone I knew a hemp rope finger-woven key chain with little metal beads that spelled out their names. I even made an attempt to transform a Clementine orange box into a doll bed for my niece. That Christmas, I am quite sure my sister thought I went completely nuts. In truth, my artist "crafty" ability is rather limited. (At least it is not something that I could make a career out of at any point.) But I had never tapped into that part of myself. So I was on a natural high, and I wanted to share my newfound creativity with everyone. Plus, I was enjoying the simplicity of my new surroundings. But more than that, opening to new ideas helped me to start moving out of the limiting constructs of who I defined as Milan. I was beginning to realize I was capable and deserving of so much more than what I had allowed into my life.

Sit and Stay

The universe made me sit with myself day after day, reading, creating, learning, communing with nature, and healing. Try as I might, every attempt to get a full-time job or move on was thwarted. It was clear that I was meant to just be. So that is exactly what I did. For the first time in my life, I started to feel at peace with myself. I was open to being open. My heart was mending, my faith was renewing, and my trust was building. After two years of living on seven acres in the middle of nowhere, I felt my broken wings had finally begun to heal. I was beginning to feel the need to see if I was ready to fly out into the world on my own again. Intuitively, I knew it was time because I started to feel stuck and antsy. Even my friend had been given spiritual guidance that it was soon going to be time for me to move on. But more than that, I needed to know if I could handle life again. The only real challenge I had at that point was deciding what to do and where to go. As fate would have it, the answer came to me through a friend telling me about his son's experience teaching in Korea. It sounded like the perfect solution for my next step.

I mulled the idea over for all of about what seemed like a minute. And then, out of the blue, I announced to my friend, "I am moving to South Korea to be an English teacher." In honesty, it wasn't really a statement; it was more like a tantrum, which was simply in response to getting excruciatingly restless at the Park. Bless my dear friend; she had been living with me for two years, tolerating my random comments and occasional outbursts. So in response to my announcement, she smiled and said, "Are you sure that is what you want to do?" (Although I am sure secretly she was rolling her eyes and thinking "Sure you are, honey." But if she wasn't thinking that, I am sure there was a part of me that was.) Regardless, as fate would have it, two months later with a plane ticket in hand, I was headed east. It was the beginning of the second leg of my seven-year journey that took me back to the basics in the rediscovery of human values.

> Anger is an acid that can do more harm to the vessel in which it is stored than to anything on which it is poured.
>
> —(Mark Twain, American author and humorist)

33,000 Miles (and One Oversized Bookshelf) to Get "Home"

Even before the 2002 fiasco and my time at the Park, I had been traversing the "spiritual path" for a very long time. My initial quest for answers started at an early age in response to an unstable and abusive upbringing. My life rotated around physical, verbal, and sexual abuse, neglect, and at times downright emotional torture. It was almost as if I was hated from the beginning. I wasn't planned. I was merely the result of a tryst that transpired in the back of a 1967 Pontiac which ended with a forged marriage between two mismatched souls. My mother was young and wounded by her own childhood. My father was conflicted with a psychological issue that centered on gender identity. There was no real love between my parents. In fact, my mother hated my father and was embarrassed by his issues. As a result of major discord, personal problems, and simply not loving each other, they divorced only a few, short years later. In an effort to continue to hurt each other, they used the only trump card they had—me. Finally frustrated with my mother's antics, my father abandoned me. My mother had won her (perceived) battle at the cost of my happiness and a relationship with my father.

Not knowing any better, she redirected all her pent-up anger and resentment toward me. In her eyes, I was the "mistake" that kept her from getting the life she deserved. To her, I was disposable. As I found out much later in life, it was the same way that she had been treated by her mother. Since she was living without conscious awareness, she allowed every boyfriend, friend, or husband to treat me as they pleased. Growing up, it wasn't unusual to see the social worker at our door. However, when they did come around, she would have a million convincing excuses as to why she had to discipline such an unruly child. It was also a time when corporal punishment was more readily overlooked.

In an attempt to cope with my pain, my body started shutting down. I also started having vivid dreams that were premonitions of abuse that would come a day or two later. In hindsight, I feel that it was a gift to help me survive the reality since I had already had the experience in dreamtime. Then there was another point in time where whenever I was beaten, I would simply pass out. My little body made every effort to protect itself. By the time I was six or seven, I was already contemplating how to kill myself. It was all too much. One day, I decided that I had had enough. So I concocted a rather crude (and ineffective) way to end my life. When my mother found me, she asked me, "What the hell are you doing?" When I told her that I wanted to kill myself, she simply offered to help.

> Out of suffering have emerged the strongest souls; the most massive characters are seared with scars.
>
> —(Kahlil Gibran, poet, artist, writer)

The pain and suffering only magnified over the years. As I got older, my life started to become a piecemealed memory. I had very little recollection of my previous years. Again, it was another protective measure to aid in my survival. But my life went on. Some days good, some bad, and some horrendous. But the balance of my existence started to take a slow turn to staying on the side of unbearable. By the time I was twelve, one of my beatings took a rather grim turn for the worst. The man's rage seemed insatiable and it seemed as if he would not stop pummeling my young body. The man hurting me was very drunk and angry. I remember that night very vividly. I also recall praying for death. But God had a different plan, and I survived. There was no recourse or accountability for what happened to me. In fact, my mother never did anything to stop the abuse. She only participated in it through ignoring it or inflicting it herself.

By the time I was seventeen, I had been in seven different schools as my mother flitted to one doomed, dysfunctional relationship after another. I had no idea what it meant to have any stability in my life. Life was, at best, tumultuous. The final straw came when yet another one of my mother's boyfriends molested me. This time, I asked my mother for help. In response, my mother decided to send me to live in a group home.

Fortunately at the time, we lived in state where children could be emancipated when they were sixteen. I spoke to the group home coordinator privately in an intake interview. To this day, I can't even begin to tell you what I said to him. But he agreed that I didn't belong there. After some convincing, the group home coordinator persuaded my mother to let me go. I took my last paycheck from my after-school job and bought a one-way ticket as far as I could go. I ended up in Chicago. That was the last time I ever really saw my mother.

> There are two ways of meeting difficulties: You alter the difficulties or you alter yourself to meet them."
>
> —(Phyllis Bottome, British novelist)

An old friend from my freshman year of high school and her mother picked me up from the airport, and we headed north. My plan was to just stay with friends until I graduated from high school. However, my mother's reputation for being, shall we say, difficult blocked me at every turn. Everyone wanted to help me and see me succeed, but no one wanted to deal with my mother. Without any success, I spent over a month trying to enroll myself back into high school as well as trying to find a place to live. However, now I was living in a state where you needed a parent's permission and signature to enroll in school. There were no emancipation laws to protect or help me. And I certainly wasn't going to turn to my mother for help. Finally, a friend's family (who had not ever had the pleasure of interacting with my mother) took me in. Although kind and generous, they were not in a financial position to feed another child. Moreover, they did not have the legal right to enroll me back in school. Fortunately, after some time, my real father (who lived in the same area) found out I was wandering and took me in. I ended up finishing my senior year of high school with a 1.6 grade point average and two credits shy of the graduation requirements. But I didn't care. I was finally free!

> Sometimes I lie awake at night and ask, "Why me?" Then a voice answers, "Nothing personal, your name just happened to come up."
> —(Charles M. Schulz, American cartoonist)

Why Me?

As a child and for a long time as an adult, I couldn't understand why life dealt me what seemed to be the worst possible hand. I wandered around lost, confused, and (at times) became self-destructive. I was angry with God, myself, and my existence in general. I had nowhere to turn…not even religion. I had come from a religious background that only instilled guilt and separateness, not solace. I wanted a reprieve from the constant battering from the universe. I wanted to know why God was picking on me. I wanted answers, and I was desperate to find them at any cost.

> Most people have come to prefer certain of life's experiences and deny and reject others, unaware of the value of the hidden things that may come wrapped in plain and even ugly paper. In avoiding all pain and seeking comfort at all costs, we may be left without intimacy or compassion; in rejecting change and risk we often cheat ourselves of the quest; in denying our suffering we may never know our strength or our greatness.
>
> —(Rachel Naomi Remen, pioneer in the mind/body holistic health movement)

At first, in an effort to bury my pain, I did what most people with my history do; I went crazy and indulged in all sorts of vices to numb myself. I tried everything from binge drinking, smoking marijuana, overeating, to excessive shopping in an effort to resolve the turmoil that was constantly brewing inside. I fluttered around from random job to job and boyfriend to boyfriend. I also moved. In fact, I have relocated so much that at this point, I have lived in sixteen different states and owned more dishware sets and vacuum cleaners than anyone I know. However, as one would expect, those things that I did to numb my pain only further eroded away what was left of my life and buried me in debt and despair.

I came to quickly understand that as fun as it seemed at the time, finding myself naked and covered with a bathroom rug after a night of sake bombers was not helping me in any way whatsoever. I also learned (a bit more gradually) that renting a U-Haul every six months certainly wasn't creating any sort of stability in my life. I began to slowly realize that these coping mechanisms were not only not working but causing me a lot more trouble than necessary. No one can figure out how to be happy at the end of an empty bottle or package of cookies.

As a resolve, I tried a 180 maneuver and started dabbling in various religious dogmas. I started out with Native American teaching then ran the gamut from Wicca to Buddhism. In one last-ditch effort, I jokingly told everyone that I was part of the "Church of Milan." Granted, in the process of undertaking my pursuits, I learned a great deal of valuable life-affirming information from every teaching. However, I just made things more complicated for myself because I wasn't ready to give up all the vices that I was using to self-medicate. As such, my behavior was contradicting my new practices. I became even more conflicted. In response, I started desperately searching for more ways to get out of the loop of craziness. I was on a runaway roller coaster of negative emotion and misguided information. I didn't know how to get off and was running out of ways to exit from my pain. I was frantic to find any resolve (and the quicker the better). So somewhere in between the binge drinking and religious philosophies, I would find the time to jump at the mere hint of any kind of quick-fix answer that came from whoever was the latest spiritual guru/teacher.

> I went to a bookstore and asked the saleswoman, "Where's the self-help section?" She said if she told me, it would defeat the purpose.
>
> —(George Carlin, comedian)

As an adjunct to whatever practice I was submerged in, I read an enormous amount of self-help books. I did this with the intention of trying to further help "sort myself out" or find some snippet of wisdom that would end my perpetual suffering. As it is with some of the things we read, oftentimes the information would not resonate with me. Other times I got lucky, and I would get an (albeit) temporary sense of well-being as if I finally stumbled upon "the answer." It was like a high to feel like I finally "got it." But these answers always had an expiration date, and like sour milk in the fridge, it ended up stinking. So I had no choice but to throw it out and start again.

Since I was convinced that my self-worth and happiness were both tied to some external variable, if all that extraneous stuff wasn't enough, just for good measure, I completed enough college education to satisfy three people. I did all of it to insure that I had covered all my bases. I also had an overwhelming need to have people see me as smart. There was also an inner five-year-old fighting back in response to my father telling me that I "didn't need a master's degree. All I need was to come home and get a good waitressing job." In response to such a ludicrous statement, my petulant inner child dug her heels in and shouted, "I'll show you!" Her outburst ended up costing me around

$112,000 in student loan debt. The irony is that I didn't really feel any smarter, much less satisfied with my life. I only felt eternally indebted to the loan agency.

> I hope life isn't a big joke, because I don't get it.
> —(Jack Handey, American fictional humorist)

And the Oscar Goes To…

Of course, it wasn't until after the fact that I came to realize that papering my walls with certificates and diplomas only made me "look" more together than I really was. By the end of my education pursuits, I had a bachelor's in psychology and metaphysics, half a master's in social work, and a master's in education counseling and metaphysics as well as a doctorate in spiritual counseling.

I came to find out very quickly that being overeducated is a very difficult façade to maintain. My walls didn't match how I really saw myself or how smart I actually felt. As such, I felt like I was constantly on stage, standing under a hot spotlight. I spent an inordinate amount of time being scared that eventually someone would see me for the train wreck that I thought I was. As I result, I felt I had to play different roles with the people around me. The paradox is that none of those personas were really me. In fact, I had no idea who I really was because I was so lost in the illusion of being what I thought everyone wanted me to be or what I thought I should be.

Where was the darn director to yell "Cut"? Pretending to be anyone but who you are is wearing. Yet I just could not logically see how allowing myself to be a walking disaster would be beneficial to anyone. In retrospect, I need to give credit where credit is due. I was really good at living a lie. And the Oscar goes to Milan Hollister for Best Supporting Actress in the role of *Her Life*. This is also where moving around the country came in handy. I was able to constantly reinvent myself to keep up the different façades. However, I knew I couldn't keep up the charade forever. At some point, I had to stop hiding from myself. But, I didn't know what to do or how to stop the madness.

So after a lot of soul-searching, I gave myself a self-diagnosis. I decided that I had what I call spiritual self-help ADD. I simply was unable to focus on any one healing modality. I was like a crow (or barracuda), easily distracted by anything sparkly. Every journey, persona, and/or answer I embarked upon was very short-lived. I had an inability to really concentrate on any one thing, and being grounded was a totally foreign concept. At the time, this wasn't exactly helpful information. It simply gave me another excuse to cling on to my lies until I could really "find the answer." But it was a first pass at admitting that I had a problem.

The challenge with my life was that living in a lie was exhausting. I was so tired. I also knew I didn't want to be here anymore. I didn't even know what that feeling meant. I just knew that I deeply longed to go somewhere else. I wanted to be free. However, I didn't have a clue as to where or what that was. It wasn't until my mid-thirties that I was finally set on a direct course toward home and *back to the basics*.

> "Never confuse movement with action."
> —(Ernest Hemingway, writer)

Easier Said Than Done

Before my "real" epiphany came to me (the values), try as I might, most of the information that seemed to be the answer or theoretically easy to understand always seemed to get lost somewhere between the pages of the book and the application of the concepts. What I tended to lack was one very important piece: the ability to simply do it or to make the long-term commitment, which seems to be a vital component for completing most of the self-help prescriptions. The theories would stick for a while, sometimes days, or if I was very lucky, a month or two. But every practice ended with the same results—typically that was buying another self-help book! Then there were times when I didn't have the money to buy books. During those periods, I became a permanent fixture between rows at Barnes & Nobles as I tried to absorb as much information as I could from the vast collection of books offering to "help." Now I had a new addiction to alleviate my pain—self-help remedies.

After extracting every snippet of wisdom, the results were always the same. I continued to unceasingly feel that my life was missing something. But even with all the self-guidance prescriptions, I had no idea what that something was. This lack put me on what seemed like an unending quest for answers. In my effort to fill the void, I developed a voracious appetite for solutions to what seemed to be an insurmountable list of questions. In an attempt to quell the feelings, I studied nearly everything that I could get my hands on. So not only did I end up with a lot of education, I can't even begin to tell you about the incalculable certification courses and lectures that I have attended.

I studied everything from self-acupuncture, naturopathic health, energy healing to quantum physics. In addition to my education, I became a Life Coach, a Reverand, and a Reiki Masters. I tried to learn everything and do it all. The funny thing is that I have never really used anything that I learned. I'm sure it might come up from time to time. But nothing has stuck as a passion or primary focus. I mean, let's face it, self-acupuncture is a little unnerving. I could potentially prick myself in the wrong place and end up with some strange kind of paralysis. As for the quantum physics, although interesting, try talking about that with someone and see if they call you again to chat over coffee. I was missing the core point of existence. I was not living in alignment with love, truth, peace, right conduct, and nonviolence.

> Any man who reads too much and uses his own brain too little falls into lazy habits of thinking.
> —(Albert Einstein, physicist)

All the classes, compounded by the enormous amount of information that I extracted from the books I had read, only left me feeling emptier, more confused, a little bit frustrated, and no more "enlightened" than I was before I started on my journey. If anything, I started feeling like I knew too much about nothing in particular. This only manifested a new complication. Now I had way more information rattling around in my head than I needed. Furthermore, I started to get confused about what and who was right. Moreover, I had no clear idea about which path to chose. So in addition to having the issues that I started with, now I felt guilt and inadequacy for not being smart enough or spiritual enough to sort myself out. I mean, according to the experts, it was all super easy to do. The recipes were all so simple, and the messages started to repeat themselves. Theoretically, no one was really suggesting anything new or inventive. In principle nothing seemed overtly complicated. So what was my problem?

One Too Many Passport Stamps

> Life only demands from you the strength you possess. Only one feat is possible—not to have run away.
>
> —Dag Hammarskjöld (Diplomat)

When All Else Fails, Update Your Passport

As each of my self-help routes failed, I resorted to wandering. That is really just a polite way of saying avoiding my issues. But you say potato, I say patato. I have spent so much money and time trying to find myself that if I would have had the forethought, I could have platinum status frequent flyers miles. Ah… If only my life could in some way be retroactive! Just think about the mileage perks! Over the last twenty years, I have moved around to sixteen states, visited another fourteen countries, and lived abroad in four countries, always looking for myself and trying to free myself from myself at the same time. That's a lot of time spent in a U-Haul and/or coach seating. In fact, I have done so much traveling that I've had to have pages added to my passport.

So here is what I learned from all that moving around: it doesn't work simply because "I" was there the whole time. No matter where I went, there "I" was. The paradox was that what I wanted and what I was trying to escape from were all locked within me (and having quite a battle, I might add). As it turned out, I didn't need a passport. I needed a mirror and some restraint.

> The first rule of holes: when you're in one, stop digging.
>
> —(Molly Ivins, writer)

If That Doesn't Work, Join a Cult

Since moving around wasn't curing what ailed me, in one of my final, last-ditch efforts of desperation, while living in Korea, I went so far as to join what I will gently qualify as a "meditation group." They offered a very direct and quick way to alleviate my suffering—breathing. Yes, it sounds rather fundamental. But their way was supposed to be the fast-track to inner peace. All I could think was "sign me up."

Although the initiation fee was a whopping $1,000 (with $80 monthly dues), it took me less than an hour to withdraw the money from my bank account and sign up with the group. In my eyes, it seemed like a real bargain for the promised lightening-fast route to lasting bliss. In addition to guaranteed inner solace, the $1,000 came with a pajama-type uniform, a meditation pillow, and an invisible antenna attached to my head that linked me to the leader of the group who gave me "secret knowledge" (only accessed by the paid members).

> Despite the success of cults, men are most deeply moved not by the reaching of the goal but by the grandness of the effort involved in getting there—or failing to get there.
>
> —(Max Lerner, American journalist)

It took several months, but eventually, I finally came to realize that this group was nothing more than a well-intentioned cult. *Well-intentioned* and *cult* may seem like an oxymoron, but I do believe that some of the members genuinely wanted to help us "lost souls" ease the pain and suffering from our lives; it just didn't work as they planned. In a short period of time, many of the leaders from that group started to act like they were an overprivileged spiritual society. As a result, they demanded complete devotion to their agenda and total focus on the invisible "ball of power" that they thought each person developed and nurtured in their lower abdomen through the power of breathe.

Now I am sure you are wondering why or how I didn't see that earlier given the line about the pajamas, secrets, and the "invisible antenna." But it is a simple answer: I was so desperate for relief from my agony that I was willing to overlook the obvious to put an end to my suffering. As odd as this behavior may seem, I am not the first person (nor will I be the last) to make radical (and in this case ridiculous) choices as a tradeoff for hope. We all do it at some point. If it isn't a cult, it's a cream, a pill, a book, an affair, or whatever. Each of us has bought into a lie that promised up thinner thighs, cleaner floors, erased wrinkles, or in my case, an end to my perpetual suffering. No matter who we are, we are all looking for some sort of resolution for a nagging problem. Yet the real truth is that we are all just trying to meet some very core need to make ourselves feel a certain way. Most of us have the same root goals/needs... find our way back to love while feeling safe and secure. And as a rule, we will go to great lengths to extract even a glimmer of either of those feelings. As simple as those things may sound, it is really what we all strive to have in our lives in one form or another. The challenge is that most of us have beome sorely misguided regarding how to get back to those basic constructs.

Truth be told, the cult probably wasn't my last effort. It was perhaps just my weirdest. I have joined up with many different groups throughout my travels that offered up some glimmer of hope. I've taken classes to heal and balance myself with crystals; I've sat through seminars on communication, learned breathing practices from India, tried Buddhist walking meditations, taken yoga, juicing classes, Reiki training, and on and on. Each time, I went into these experiences, I went in with optimism and assuredness that "this time" I found my answer. It is almost embarrassing to look back and think about or admit all the money and time I have spent on quick fixes. To show for my efforts, I have a medicine cabinet full of miracle creams and a résumé littered with credentials. As you can imagine, the results of nearly every venture were all the same—none of them panned out or gave me a long-term resolution to my impending issues. However, as I suggested, I am hardly unique. Everyone is looking to change something. As Anthony Robbins once said, "Change is never a matter of ability. It is a matter of motivation and drive." But I will take that quote even one step further. We also need to understand why and what we need to change.

> It is good for me that I have been afflicted, that I may learn Your statutes.
>
> Psalm 119:71

It Hurts So Much, I'll Try Anything

As is human nature, for whatever reason, when a person is in crisis, they (as I did) tend to ask, "Why?" in some form or another. In the quest to find the answer to that most seemingly simplistic question, some people may do the unthinkable, irrational, and even absurd. In point of fact, I don't know too many people who, at some point in their lives, have not said aloud or thought to themselves, "Umm, I wish I wouldn't have done that." The challenge is that most people tend to look for answers on the periphery and rarely delve in and really try to extract the root cause of their pain and suffering.

Occasionally in our quest for answers, we do what some might qualify as a "dumb thing," and that's okay.

It is part of the process of finding out who we are and the value structure that we want to subscribe to. I have also learned that when you make what some (or yourself) may qualify as a mistake, you just need to brush yourself off and move on. You can certainly beat yourself up over it and continue to look over your shoulder at the past by reliving, rehashing, and running through your list of "if onlys." In the long run, it won't help anything get resolved. Trust me when I tell you I have mastered the art of self-judgment. However, when we do that to ourselves, we miss all the good that is in front of and around us. We also stay stuck and stagnant in our progression toward living a life of true happiness. As Master Oogway said in *Kung Fu Panda*, "Yesterday is history, tomorrow is a mystery. But today is a gift. That is why it is called the present." Although this saying has some very old roots, it is still pretty profound knowledge from a cartoon turtle.

> Failure is only the opportunity to begin again,
> only this time more wisely.
> —(Henry Ford, American industrialist)

Those Were All Failures…or Were They?

The questions that I had to ask myself were, "Am I really a huge failure?" Were my negative, self-loathing thoughts about my life, which was alternately defined as a train wreck, true? Were my parents correct about me? Did I have no more significance than a grain of sand? Did my perceived mistakes define my past, present, and future?

> "Live your life as though everything is rigged in your favor."
>
> – Rumi

What I came to understand was that I had not failed or wasted my time as such because each "self-help" journey, class, degree, silly decision, momentous mistake, etc., brought me closer to shining a light upon and finding what was already available to me. So no, my father was not correct. I (and my life) are much more significant than sand. But in a bit of twisted logic, he was correct from the perspective that our bodies are merely temporary vehicles and we should not become attached to the outer reality. What is important is my true inner nature. This is the part of me that is so profound that it becomes more than simply significant because it is the essence of God. So although he wasn't exactly on the money, years later, that conversation gave me cause to pause.

It turned out that the annoying metaphor about pain equating to progress did end up making some sense after all. All the drama, tears, and heartache had brought me growth. They led me from identifying with the false perception of who I really was to the "I am." My journey was really quite profound. If I really looked at who I was and the person I was becoming, I was metamorphozing from a dark cocoon into a bright, beautiful butterfly.

Truth be told, even the cult group opened my eyes to the power of the breath, commitment, and the value of good breathing techniques. What I have learned is that it isn't about what happens in our lives. It is about how we choose to interpret our situations. That is really the only free will we have. It is the thought and mental energy that we give to our extraneous environmental variables. Stress and pain only come when we give far more weight and credibility to people and our life circumstances than is really necessary.

All my successes have been built on my failures.
—(Benjamin Disraeli, British prime minister)

Everything Happens for a Reason

As I look back, I realize that every piece of my life has played an intricate part in the role of my development. Every comment, experience, failure, tragedy, success, degree, etc., has in some way been a substantial part of my growth. In fact, as I continue to grow, the universe seems to set me up for lessons that I need the most. Often times people view these trials and tribulations as road blocks. This is not true. They are grant opportunities to continue to weed through the illusion of who you are and how you have defined yourself. And as I have come to realize, I am not allowed to be "comfortable" for long. Lessons are like the rising of the sun. Regardless of whether or not you are ready, it is going to happen.

As an example of one of my more poignant lessons, a while back, I met a nice man. In fact, I was convinced very early on that he might be "the one." We met at a conference and hit it off immediately. He lived in a different state, but we kept in contact. The more we talked, the more smitten I became as we seemed to be on the same page regarding a lot of the important issues. Eventually, he invited me to come meet him for a long weekend. I was so excited. I was sure it was going to be the beginning of a beautiful and lasting relationship.

About a day or so before I was set to leave to visit him, I started to get very anxious. I was so nervous that I found myself in tears. I could not seem to help myself. Then to make matters worse, I started judging my emotions, which in turn led to anger. By the time I got on the plane to go, I was an emotional wreck. To add insult to injury, the plane was delayed, I got stuck in an awful seat, and I could not do the work for my job that I needed to get done before arriving. So I landed angry, frustrated, emotional, and guarded. I went from being ecstatic to enraged. My anger turned to judgment of myself and my actions. And as mirrors go, I reflected that judgment on to him. I knew that everything I was doing, saying, and thinking was not who I really was, but I could not seem to stop myself. It was like I had been possessed. And in reality, I was. I had been taken over by my false self (ego). But the whole experience (down to my inability to connect to WIFI on the plane) was a setup that led me to one of the greatest lessons I have ever learned.

I returned home after that five days and continued to identify with the false self that was wallowing in fear and doubt. I knew exactly what I had done. I also knew that if I stopped and assessed the situation, I would find there was a great lesson to be extracted from all of it. I just needed time to sit with all the emotions. As a result of what I said and how I acted, the man stopped communicating with me (and rightfully so). But it wasn't until he pulled away that I really delved in and spent time reflecting on my actions, words, life, and relationships that were not just related to him, but all the years that proceeded that moment. I came to the realization that in my nearly forty years, I had never truly opened my heart to anyone, not one single person—not even my dear friend from the Park.

I had never really realized that I was still so attached to my false self and willing to do or say anything to protect it. Hence, I kept my heart closed and guarded, unable to fully express or feel love. I came to understand that I had spent a lot of time walking away from people before they were able to move toward me. I had old tapes playing that told me relationships and people weren't safe and would eventually hurt me given enough time. My first rule of survival was to never get close enough or to be completely vulnerable. The only innocent people were the broken people because in my mind, I perceived them as needing me. This grossly misguided insight led me to a slew of dysfunctional relationships and more heart-break which only further contributed to my lack of self-worth and faith in love.

In order to overcome this tremendous, painful yet insightful lesson, I had to do a lot of introspection, heart-healing work, and reflection. It wasn't until I dug in, unearthed my past, and did the work to make the changes that I had the most amazing transformative, freeing, life-altering experience. For once in my life, I could finally say that I got it. I really, really got it, and my heart was open, extremely open, for the first time in my life. I came to realize that I could have never truly loved that man, myself, or anyone without this understanding and vulnerability. What's more, I could not have effectively taught the concept of love if I was incapable of having the heart space for love. That is why all that stuff needed to happen.

The universe had set me up so that I could learn one of the most important, meaningful lessons of my life. I would never have really looked at that shadow side of myself, nor would I have made an effort to identify my heart-closing behaviors if it weren't for him. It was my connection and attraction to him that made it all possible. It was my intense desire to really want to open myself and my heart that led me back to me. In the end, although he wasn't anything that I perceived him to be, he was the catalyst for a monumentous shift in my heart space. And for that I will be eternally grateful. However excruciating the lesson, it was a gift more precious than words can describe.

As it came to be in my lesson, it would seem that discomfort and strife can bring the greatest amount of growth. As in the quote mentioned at the beginning of this book, it was really only the grief and pain from my life that led me to me—the essence and embodiment of the five basic human values of love, truth, peace, right conduct, and nonviolence.

The Values

I have found that when these values are used with sincerity and determined commitment, they can unlock our greatest potential as humans, freeing us from confusion, the illusions of the world, and constrictions of our thinking mind. But more than that, they can help each and every one of us bypass an inordinate amount of pain and suffering. Disaster does not necessarily need to strike before we can see our way toward a life of peace and contentment. We don't need an antennae or miracle cream. The five human values are the essence of God, Spirit, or however you define the divine. In my personal story, it was those moments of misfortune where I found my strength. But pain and suffering doesn't need to be everyone's story or way to learn the lessons of life. We can be physically and emotionally happy now. There is an easier way to navigate life: love, truth, peace, right conduct, and nonviolence.

> If you keep thinking about what you want to do or what you hope will happen, you won't do it and it won't happen.
> —(Desiderius Erasmus, humanist and scholar)

The Values Belong to You

Looking back, my introduction to these values came early on as a child in the form of religious doctrine. As a general outline, they were first given to me as the Ten Commandments. But they were quickly lost in the cracks of fear that met somewhere in between the threat of purgatory and hell. As an adult, they were shown to me basic universal principles of how to live. At first, I only saw them as a further attempt to repair the remaining fragments of my broken identity. As such, in the beginning, the values (although seemingly simple) seemed as elusive and unobtainable as a date with Gerard Butler. But that limiting belief would begin to change as I made an effort to open myself to the concepts.

One Ticket to London, Please

In response to my further quest for relief and knowledge, I decided to learn all that I could about these values. In my quest for understanding, I found out about a course that taught the information more in-depth. The course was outside London. I signed up for the nine-day retreat and was off to England to the British Institute of Sathya Sai Education where they offered a complete values training course. Yes, there is a class where we can learn how to be good moral individuals. And as unusual as it may sound, I think it should be as mandatory as taking a driver's test for your license.

Truth be told, in response to these gallant efforts to be a more morally astute, I was sort of hoping that I would be initiated into some exclusive values club, which only allowed membership to patron saints and the righteous. (That would certainly have cleared up some loose ends I had with God.) Of course as you can guess, it didn't quite work out that way. But I did learn some very valuable and life-affirming information as well as a great deal more about each of the values.

However, the course didn't only teach me more about the values, but it reaffirmed what I had learned about the inherent oneness of all and the omnipotence of God. This idea is highlighted by the teaching of Sathya Sai Baba, a guru from India and the inspiration behind the course. He said.

> There is only one religion, the religion of Love;
>
> There is only one language, the language of the Heart;
>
> There is only one caste, the caste of Humanity;
>
> There is only one law, the law of Karma;
>
> There is only one God, He is Omnipresent.
>
> True devotion must not get dispirited; nor elated or satisfied with lesser gains; it must fight against failure, loss, calumny, calamity, ridicule and against egoism and pride, impatience and cowardice.
>
> Let the different faiths exist, let them flourish, let the glory of God be sung in all languages in a variety of tunes. That should be

> the ideal. Respect the differences between the faiths and recognize them as valid so far as they do not extinguish the flame of unity.
>
> —Sathya Sai Baba (Indian guru, spiritual figure, and educator)

For me, these words were just what I needed to piece together some dangling and fragmented ends that were taking up space in my mind. There was finally a solace in knowing that I didn't need a specific religious dogma to be complete. I could renew my faith in God without pressure or guilt and wholeheartedly immerse myself in the values to find my way back to the real me and my connection to the divine.

Even though I was hoping for a merit badge for my efforts to further understand how to be a better person, what I found was that these values are not exclusive to me or a select few. They also weren't as elusive as I first thought. In fact, they are readily available to everyone at every moment as they are innate characteristics that are inside each and every one of us. They are the fundamental nature of all human beings. They are our inner divinity that radiates outward and reminds us of the God within each and every one of us. These values are as close to us as our own hearts. They are the reflection we see in the mirror. They are the core of our existence and the pathway to all that we aspire to be—happy, healthy, and free from the mental chatter that moves us from one mundane problem the next. They are the breath of life, love, and divinity.

> Life is change. Growth is optional. Choose wisely.
>
> —Karen Kaiser Clark (Motivational Speaker)

The challenge (as with most spiritual concepts) is recognizing our innateness, extracting all the good that which we have available to us, and using the tools to effectively navigate through life. Is it easier said than done? Yes, maybe, but not by any means impossible. Change is like making a snowball. In essence, you just need one tiny snowflake to start. Then you add another and another until you have molded thousands of snowflakes into a perfectly round sphere. With change, you need the seed of desire that you can mold into progress and, ultimately, growth.

Human Values

There is only one religion, the religion of love.
—Sathya Sai Baba
(Indian guru, spiritual figure, and educator)

Are These Values Related to a Specific Religious Dogma?

Human values are related to everything. They are the foundation upon which most of our societal laws are built. And if you think about it, the values are also the basis of the Ten Commandments, which many religious dogmas subscribe to in some form or another. But no matter what the religion or practice, each one has a moral basis that relates to human values. Sathya Sai Baba (Indian spiritual figure) wrote this explanation that I feel is fitting to address this topic. He said,

> The truth proclaimed by all religions is one and the same. All religions have a common ultimate goal. All religions aim at promoting religious conduct by transforming the mental attitude of man, thereby bringing about harmony of the body, mind, and intellect. The foundation of all religions is morality. Morality is equated with selfless love. Religions were thus instituted to foster the wellbeing of society through the promotion of love for all beings. All religions advocate their votaries to seek eternal peace within oneself. No religion approves of the use of violence. Every religion recommends that cultivation of tolerance and respect for the other religions, thus paving the way for nonviolence.

So, no, human values have nothing to do with a specific religion. They are a way to live no matter who you are or what you believe, practice, or follow. They are a moral compass that can guide each and every one of us in the same positive, life-affirming direction. They can direct all of us to a metaphorical place called Love Street located in harmony, which is found in the state of peace. It's not a hard place to find if you have the right navigation tools: the five human values.

Even miracles take a little time.

—(Anonymous)

How Quickly Can Someone Change Using the Values?

Although we are a society that tends to look for and relish things that are quick and concise, there are really no quick-fix solutions in life. Reciting a mantra or incorporating a set of values into your life is not a magic trick. The end of understanding and applying any practice or theory is simply and completely up to each individual person. You have to put in the work if you really want to make positive permanent changes in your life. Change means being committed to your evolution and spiritual growth. It means not just wanting to be different, but making a solemn vow to work toward transformation.

As with everything we encounter, sometimes people are ready for the information, and others may need a little more time to absorb the concepts as they may be a drastic adjustment from where they are currently in their thinking or stage of life. But remember, good, bad, or indifferent, no matter where you are, you are exactly where you are meant to be. As such, you need to start where you are in life. The point is that it is important not to judge yourself or those around you for we are all at different places in our evolutionary journey. I remind people that if you happen to be a (metaphoric) university student, you can't expect a 3rd grader to have a sophisticated discussion about Macbeth with you. You have to meet people (and yourself) where you are in life. It is best to start running the values race at your own pace. Change is difficult and not for the faint-hearted.

> I believe that we are here for each other, not against each other. Everything comes from an understanding that you are a gift in my life—whoever you are, whatever our differences.
>
> —(John Denver, singer and songwriter)

Morocco

During my radical efforts to fill my passport with entry stamps, I was living off and on in Madrid, Spain. One weekend on a whim, I decided to head to Morocco. During my trip, I was reminded that the depth of our differences is not that far off when I was wandering through the streets of Marrakesh.

In Marrakesh, there is a large market area where you can buy just about anything you'd like (from jewels to goat's heads). There are also snake charmers and other tourist attractions. As I was walking around the market taking in all the sights, sounds, and pungent smells, I saw a man who had several monkeys stuffed into tiny little metal boxes. The boxes were far too small for the monkeys to be comfortable. All you could see was their tiny little faces peeking through the bars, looking absolutely miserable. Next to the boxes, the man had one of the monkeys out. He had the monkey on a leash, wearing a heavy metal collar. The man was tugging him along, trying to get tourists to pose with him. The monkey was holding the collar with his little hand and clearly looked in pain and distress. I was mortified by the animal cruelty I was witnessing. All I could do was stare in shock. However, the man mistook my interest as an opportunity to make money and started to come toward me. So I did the only thing any sane animal lover would do: I starting pointing at the monkey and shouting at him. However, the only English word that I could think of that translated into French was *horrible*. So here I was in the market shouting, "Horrible, horrible!" and making weird, distorted, crazy faces. He looked at me without a second glance of remorse. In fact, he looked clearly entertained by my antics. As he was judging me, I was most certain he was a sociopath. I was so angry at him but even more perturbed that civilized tourists would stop to support such wretched behavior!

Clearly, I disagreed with the man's and tourists' actions. The whole incident elicited a lot of emotion on my part that was initially retold as an account of a horrible, inhumane man that I witnessed in Morocco. And although, I still don't agree with animal cruelty of any kind, what I came to terms with later was each individual in that market were on their own evolutionary journey (even the monkey). The situation that I encountered was more than just the dynamic between the man and the monkey. It was also something that I had to look at in relation to myself. In point of fact, there had been times in my life where I made choices that could have been construed as unethical or wrong by those around me. I had also lived my life in a self-imposed bondage. Metaphorically speaking, like the monkey, I, too, had tended to walk around "shackled" by my own fear and unwillingness to love myself, open my heart, and live my life to the fullest. In the past, I had also confined myself to a box that was far too small to allow myself to breath and live to my greatest potential.

So the real lesson wasn't about the ethical treatment of animals. It was for me to step out of my false self and identify the heart-closing behaviors that I had imposed upon myself. It was an opportunity for me to reconnect from a heart space. As Sathya Sai Baba once said, "All that you see is a reflection of what is inside of you. If you call a person bad, it is just that the bad in you is reflected in him. It has got nothing to do with him. Good and bad are reflections of your inner being. Never consider that good and bad are separate from you." There is a quote that sums this up simply and perfectly. It says, "We don't see things as they are. We see them as we are."

> When we are no longer able to change a situation–we are challenged to change ourselves.
> —(Viktor E. Frankl, Austrian neurologist and psychiatrist as well as a Holocaust survivor)

No matter what is going on in front of us or around us, it is important to keep in mind that no one's position in this world is better or more right. This idea is the epitome of the concept related to being nonjudgmental. We should work to remember that everyone is part of an intricate puzzle that creates what we interpret as "reality." What we are seeing around us is simply a reflection of our own inner making. According to the laws of quantum physics, everyone and everything in your reality is what you have created. So when you judge what is around you, you are really just judging yourself. This is a concept that I will address in more detail later on in the book.

To start out on the path, in addition to all the other bits, anything we want to successfully embark upon takes focus, commitment, and integrity, which requires someone to have complete alignment with their thoughts, words, and actions. There is a strange cyclical logic that requires you to call on your values to practice the values. The concept is as simple as "think before you act." Or in this case, review your values before taking any action. What would be the point of smiling at someone and wishing them well only to curse them as soon as they walked by you? This is a simple example of not being in complete alignment.

If Change Were Easy, Everyone Would Do It

Now naturally, at times, all this value business can seem like an insurmountable challenge. This is why there are a lot of people on the planet unwilling to change and prefer to live a life of, at best, complacency. I know a lot of people that live exactly in this way. It is sad to witness. But again, change is rarely ever easy. I think I can even fairly say it is really hard work. It takes time, often a lifetime. Yet as the great inventor Henry Ford once said, "If you think you can do a thing or think you can't do a thing, either way, you're right." The good news is that the sheer fact that you are willing to read a book about values is a step in the right direction. "A journey of a million miles begins with one single step" (Lao Tzu, father of Taoism).

> The key to change... is to let go of fear.
>
> —(Rosanne Cash, daughter of American singer Johnny Cash)

Fear Is Our Greatest Nemesis

I am not afraid of a lot of things. I can easily handle spiders, major life changes, and monsters under the bed. But some of the things that I have been afraid of—like commitment, love, and trust—have been known to take me to my knees or take my mind to a place where Stephen King wouldn't even want to visit. Fear can be a game changer in one's life. It is so powerful that just when you think something is going well, fear can rear its ugly head, and in an instant, something that was once seemingly pleasant or even normal turns dreadful and crippling. Fear can take someone's love, goals, and faith and twist them until there is nothing more left than the broken pieces of what was once hope.

The thing about fear is that people are rarely equipped to completely eradicate it. Typically, the best we can do is acknowledge our fears and then just be present with them, trying not to allow them to completely consume us. However, once we are present with fear, it is easier to disassociate with the limiting or heart-closing belief that prompted the feeling. Dr. John Goldthwait (2007) explained it in this way: "When you become nonattached to something that has closed your heart and you let it go, your heart spontaneously opens and your experience of whatever you had closed your heart to transforms."

In essence, fear can never take from you what you are unwilling to give it. They key is to not attach to the fear and to open our hearts and move toward a place and space of love. But for many, fear becomes the enemy because we allow it to take us over, and we end up giving over to its control. It cripples us when it dictates our lives and stifles our dreams. Then just for good measure, the fear shows ourselves and the world a shadowy, dark, unhappy side of who we are—not our truth (inner divinity). Ironically, most of the fears that we have are about things that have yet to happen (and probably never will).

Imagining the Worst

A woman I knew was seriously fretting over her future with her boyfriend. She kept creating scenarios about what could happen in their relationship. She kept talking about what if he got tired of her? What if he found someone else? What if he wasn't "the one?" What if she stayed with him and then ended up unhappy at some arbitrary point in the future? She had herself so wrapped up in these imagined situations that she was sabotaging a perfectly good relationship. But she continued to really work herself up over all the potential scenarios.

Her fear of things not working out became so overwhelming and lifelike that she was consumed with thinking about breaking up with her boyfriend based on things that had never even happened (and more than likely wouldn't). She was constantly playing the "what if he" game. I tried to gently remind her that she was letting her imagination get the best of her and that maybe it was time to stop and see where she was in the relationship at that moment. However, she became completely caught up in her head and stopped loving with her heart. As a result, so invested in her thoughts of "what could happen," several months later, out of fear, she finally broke off the relationship. As you can imagine, she was heartbroken that things didn't work out. But she had convinced herself of an inevitable course of doom and gloom and was unwilling to let go of her abysmal thoughts. Hence, in her mind, she had no choice but to end things with him. That is the irony as well as the ugly power of fear.

In fairness, I could easy insert my name into a similar story relating to an overworked imagination. I have bailed out on or sabotaged my fair share of relationships before I would bear the brunt of my own imagination. I had been the master at the "what if" game. In fact, if it were ever to have become an Olympic sport, I could have been a gold medal champion. But that is the way that fear works for most people. We project ourselves into the future and let our imaginations run away with us as we conjure up a laundry list of fear-based what ifs. The end result is always the same. We fail, thus confirming our fears and keeping us stuck in the endless cycle of fear.

In my personal past, there probably wasn't a week that went by without my thoughts getting the best of me. Even now, I quite often have to reel my mind back in and remind it that there is a time and place to think. Then in instances where fear has won a battle, I have to sit myself down, assess why the fear cropped up, do some damage control, and evaluate how I am going to win the war. Working with deep-seated fears can take conscious awareness, time, and patience. It isn't always easy to erase old fear tapes all in one go. Yet it must be done in order to keep some semblance of sanity, order, and balance in our lives. But the fact of the matter is simply this: "Fear is the worse use of the imagination" (Sathya Sai Baba).

> To conquer our fears is the beginning of wisdom.
>
> —(Bertrand Russell, British philosopher)

It's Not All That Bad—Is It?

Here's my take on all of this. I don't think that there is anything wrong with being afraid from time to time. I liked to simply think of (some) fears as an extreme way our unconsciousness gets our attention. Sometimes, we need our fight-or-flight mechanism intact to safely navigate life until we have complete, unadulterated faith in the divine. Until then, without fear, we'd all be standing in line to bungee jump without the retracting rope. So here is what I suggest: embrace fears as they can be great teachers. If we can take time to just sit with our fears and try to understand them, then we have the opportunity to find the massive amount of hidden wisdom that is buried beneath the surface of the problem (fear). Once we have it uncovered and can look at it as the objective viewer, it can open our heart, bringing us back toward our divine potential. In essence, fear can be viewed as positive as long as we keep it in perspective. The trick to that is we just need to remember that we are *not* the fear!

It is also important to remember that underlying all fear is the belief that we are separate, alone, and powerless. But that is only the ego talking; it is not our truth. The truth of who we are is so much more powerful than our fears! If we are immersed in the values, we can never be lost or fearful for long because we have the best GPS system in the world, the divine light that shines within—God.

> "Cheshire puss," asked Alice, "would you tell me, please, which way I ought to go from here?"
>
> "That depends a good deal on where you want to go," said the cat.
>
> "I don't much care where," said Alice.
>
> "Then it doesn't matter which way you go," said the cat.
>
> —(Charles "Lewis Carroll" Dodgson, Alice's Adventures in Wonderland)

Okay, So What Exactly Are Human Values?

The concepts of human values may seem simple enough. Yet for whatever reason, in our day-to-day existence, we have lost the core, deeper meaning of love, truth, peace, right conduct, and nonviolence. As a society or an individual, some may think that they have those things in order within themselves. But the fact of the matter is that many of us don't. Many of us have lost sight of where we are really going and how we are trying to get there. We can easily trick ourselves into believing that we are more virtuous than we are. Then there are others who have no trouble stepping over or on someone to get what they want. These kinds of people would be qualified as those who simply don't care where they are treading. They are more concerned about the process of getting there and not the moral repercussions of their actions. In today's culture, many people firmly believe that you have to "take what you want from this world." We use phrases like "It's a dog eat dog world out there."

People feel they have to fight for their lives, happiness, and position in this existence. Because of this mentality and other negative thought processes, each and every day, people are making decisions out of anger, fear, frustration, and/or selfishness.

Life Is a Battlefield

I have a dear friend who, in his mind, feels he is having a tough go at life. Interestingly, if you listen to his words, he prefaces nearly every conversation he has related to his reality with "I need to win the war," "I need to fight," "It's a battle," or "I need a sword to defend myself against." He goes to the extreme with the way that he talks about his world and all the encounters he faces. It is his rationale that is creating a life filled with strife and hardship. His perception of life has become grossly skewed. His words have kept him stuck as his mind is unable to imagine a world full or miracle and possibilities. Furthermore, he uses the turmoil and strife from the outside world to reinforce his negative beliefs. So, he is put himself in a lose, lose situation. There is no place for him to turn to find sanctuary or solace from his own mind. He isn't alone in his thinking about how people believe they are waging a war against life; he's just more verbally descriptive. In fact, on day to day, I hear about people who truly feel that they need some kind of literal or figurative arsenal to navigate this (perceived) big, bad, cold, scary world.

Some people have become zombies in their lives, just moving forward dead, unawake, unaware, and hungry for more. There are some who stay immersed in political turmoil, complaining and toiling over things that really don't have as much significance in their lives as they would like to believe. If someone (or a collective) is waiting for one person or a group of people to create some miaculumlous change in the way things are happening in this world, they are missing the bigger picture and the smaller point. Beyond that, there are others who truly believe that all they have in life is their work, family, children, house, car, etc. They can't discern the forest from the trees. They end up defining themselves with by what they do, the watch they wear, the stocks they own, or the car they drive, etc. When those things go to the wayside, often times, people no longer know who they are or how they can go on. In their minds identity and worth = superfluous stuff. But no matter what we believe, those things aren't all that anyone has. Life is so much more than our external variables. Moreover, life is not a battle or a war to be won. It is a gift to be treasured.

How did we get to the place where we believe that our existence is nothing more than the objects that we possess? A big part of that answer is marketing, advertising, and media. But no matter where the blame lies, we are solely responsible for our own thoughts, actions, and purchases. Moreover, often times, the possessions that we value are just transitory things. Take a moment to think about all the people and stuff that have come in and out of your reality. Thanks to the advent of infomercials, home shopping networks, and

BOGO sales, we are ecstatic in one moment with our new purchase, only to find it in the back of a closet a year later, still in the box or hanging with the price tag.

It is the human values that help us to remember we have so much more inside of us than we could even begin to excude on the outside. We are so much more intelligent, capable, tuned in, aware, and divine than we can ever begin to imagine. It isn't the treasures that we possess outwardly that define who we are; it is the riches that we hold within. These are the values.

Extrinsic vs. Intrinsic Motivation

For the most part, our society (and other industrialized nations) is driven by extrinsic motivation. The goal for many is a nicer car, bigger house, newer smartphone, fame, or some other tangible motivator. The challenge with extrinsic motivators are that they are unable to fulfill people long-term. In fact, even though many people think that "money can buy happiness," in fact, it can't. What it buys is some comfort and a temporary sense of well-being. What happens more often than not is that people become attached to tangible objects to fill emotional voids. This can create a false, impermanent sense of happiness. But with all things, time erodes away at the perceived worth of what was once considered a treasured piece. Nothing on the outside can or will give you lasting value on the inside. Additionally, research has shown that extrinsic motivation can take something that could be pleasurable and quickly change it into something rather unenjoyable.

As an example, in a research study conducted by Lepper, Greene, and Nisbett (1973), they asked two groups of children to do some drawings. One group was promised a "good player medal" for their work, and the other was promised nothing. On a return visit, the groups were given paper and crayons, and what they did was observed. The results: the group who had been given a medal for drawing spent significantly less time drawing as compared to the no-reward group.

In point of fact, in order for extrinsic motivation to create any kind of long-term or meaningful happiness or be the means to long-term motivation, it must be coupled with intrinsic motivation.

Intrinsic motivation is when we do something because we enjoy it, find it pleasurable, or gives us a feeling of giving to others. It is giving love to another because love will become its own reward. It is caring for another because we have compassion in our hearts. It is going to work and knowing that the job we are doing is not just for money, but it is the responsibility, task, and talent that we have been given by the divine. Intrinsic motivation is the core values at work in our daily lives. It is the direct path to happiness as it bypasses the tangible and transient stuff and moves us to what is important—feelings, relationships, connection, and love. As humans, we need both extrinsic and intrinsic motivation. However, we need to be sure that we aren't attaching ourselves to things of temporal value and keeping the values as our moral guidance. Ask yourself questions like, "Are you truly happy with your job? Does it provide both intrinsic and extrinsic incentive for you? If not, what would you be doing?" Depak Chopra once said, "Do what you love and the money will come." Don't live another moment living a life of complacency. Do something today that your future self will thank you for and sets you on the course for more inspired, value focused living.

> Morality is not the doctrine of how we may make ourselves happy, but how we may make ourselves worthy of happiness.
>
> —(Immanuel Kant, German philosopher)

Now granted, in fairness (and realistically), it isn't always easy to hold ourselves in a space of higher moral ground all the time, much less most of the time. Besides, the way things are in the world today, it isn't always easy to feel capable, much less divine. Yet by not completely tapping into our basic value structure, we are thrown totally out of balance and denying ourselves the right to what we really deserve: love, happiness, inner peace, and what is deemed as the grand prize—enlightenment, God realization, heaven, or as some call it, bliss. As such, most of us tend to look for ways to bring ourselves back to ourselves (or center) by looking for answers on the periphery (i.e., books, lectures, counselors, etc.). However, these are only temporary fixes as once we are thrown one of the many curveballs that life gives us, we are knocked back into our outer illusion that we fondly call reality. What we know to be right and what we actually do tend to be conflicting practices.

This can be a vicious, destructive, emotional roller coaster for anyone on the planet. But more than that, it is a life that is not consistently (or ever) in alignment with practicing human values. The effect is not only felt on a personal level, but ultimately ends up impacting everything on a planetary level too. No matter how we try to put on a face when we head out into the world, the drama and confusion that is percolating within us will impact those around us. In fact, research done by Janine Willis and Alexander Todorov at Princeton University found that people make judgements about attractiveness, likeability, trustworthiness, competence, and aggressiveness after looking at a person's face for just a tenth of a second (Wood, 2012). But beyond the overt physical cues we give off, recall the last time that you just sensed something was wrong with a friend or coworker even though they didn't say a word related to any presenting issue or were even walking around with a big smile on their faces. Regardless, you just knew they had a problem or something was amiss because you "felt it." Negative emotions are like really bad body odor. Sooner or later, someone is going to smell it and wonder where it's coming from.

> A Bad Attitude is Like a Flat Tire. You Can't Go Anywhere Until You Change It.
>
> —(Author Unknown)

Rationalized Behavior: The Less Obvious Plea of Insanity

Many of us have become so good at rationalizing our behavior or living in a fog that we aren't even aware that we are not following a basic moral code. We get stuck in a rut with antiquated belief structures. Then as time passes and the farther we stray from these values, the harder it is to come back into focus. Instead of figuring out the presenting issues, for many people, it is just easier to explain and justify their actions with a reserve of excuses that could paper the sky. But what many of us fail to realize or remember is that the way we move and interact within the world says a lot about who we are as people. This concept is about more than being the token good person or holding some higher ethical standard. It is about being the living proof of what we want to see changed in the world. It is about living your life with a contentment and ease that far surpasses any mundane notion or definition of happiness. It is about a quality of existence.

Anything can change—we can change, the world can change—but it all starts within. So all of this begs the questions "What are you saying to the world and to yourself? And where do you want to go, and how do you want to get there? And do you believe that you deserve the best that life has to offer?"

I have spent the majority of my life trying to figure out the answers to these questions. Then just when I thought I had it all figured out, the universe will clearly test the foundation of my value structure. Over time (and with work), I have come to realize that I can pass most of the tests I am given. However, occasionally, that passing grade only comes on the retake exam or, in some cases, the re-retake exam. Point being, I have had my fair share of do-overs. But what I really seem to struggle with more often than not was consistently believing that I deserved the very best that life has to offer me. That is my personal reason for getting so many "pop quizzes" from the universe.

I have also done enough self-reflection to know that the root of many of my problems stemmed from my parents rejecting me. My father left me around the age of four, and my stepparents never accepted me as their own much less as a significant member of the family. And my mother not only resented me, but sold me out for a glimmer of a hope for a relationship with any man or a weekend at a dog show. With that kind of inception point, it seemed impossible to believe that anyone else could really love and accept me for me. Theoretically, if my parents could not see my value or love me, then how would anyone else? I began to believe that if I could not get people to love me, then it stood to reason that I only really deserved the leftovers of life. So my reality became a litany of rejection after rejection. My internal tape was set only to play, "You're not good enough, smart enough, pretty enough, rich enough, or thin enough" over and over throughout my life.

From there, every denial, bad job, breakup, etc., further magnified what I already believed to be true. I ended up stuck in a loop that only continued to exacerbate the idea that I didn't deserve the best and gave more fuel to my excuses for failure. I lived by the premise that the only way to be loved was to give everything I had to someone else, even if that meant martyrdom. It meant finding people who were even more broken than I was and fixing them because I could not repair myself. When those things didn't work, I simply sabotaged my relationships so that the end would come quickly, and my broken self could be right about the "awful, cruel world where no one could love me" at the expense of my happiness. Point-blank, I was unhappy because I was making myself unhappy. I had bought into the hype and the outdated concepts and labels that people had given me (or I gave myself). More than that, I was relying on my poor excuses to justify my bad behavior.

I needed to stop living with the justification that my world didn't work out because I wasn't good enough, pretty enough, smart enough, thin enough, or whatever. I had to stop trying to convince the wrong people to love and accept me. I needed to stop trying to rescue and repair everyone's life. And I most certainly needed to stop trying to fix myself. The truth is that there wasn't (and isn't) anything wrong with me. I simply needed to love myself and know to the core of my being that I am worthy. I needed to open my heart to new thoughts and really believe that I am lovable. I *am* divine. I am enough! What I needed to understand was that the right people will love me without the extra effort or convincing because they will automatically see and appreciate all that is good about me. They will show up as an equal partner and know that they too are worthy, lovable, and whole. But the only way to clear the slate and step into our truth is to live in the values that are the essence of all that is divine and the love that is within each of us. Outdated concepts are like bad fashion—there are some things you just don't wear because they don't make you look good.

> Work on yourself first, take responsibility for your own progress.
>
> —(I Ching, One of the oldest of the Chinese Classic texts)

Whose Responsibilty Is It?

Some time ago, I received the following in an email that was being forwarded around the internet. I though it was a brilliant breakdown of how to live without undo stress. The title was "It is not your business to love me, it is mine." -Byron Katie

One of Byron Katie's teachings is that in order to stay stress free, we need to remain in what is deemed as our own business. She recognized that there are only three types of businesses in this universe: Other's Business, God's Business, My Business.

What she came to observe was that most of the stress that we create in our minds are due to mentally doing other people's business. Example thoughts of being in "Other's business."

> You need to get a job
> I want you to be happy
> You should be on time
> You need to take better care of yourself
> John does not listen to me
> Julie did not smile at me
> My husband should love me more
> My children do not care for me enough

My employer should appreciate me
My mother should understand me
People should be kinder to me

According to Byron, in all the above examples, the person thinking these thoughts is linking her well being to something someone else should do and should not do, which obviously is not in her control. It is thus the other person's business to do or not do what they need to do, not ours.

Here are Byron's examples of thoughts related to being in "God's business"
I'm worried about the possible earthquake in California
I fear that the river will get flooded next year
I fear that that the world will end
When will it rain this season?
When will I die?

By Byron Katie's definition, anything that cannot be done by us or others is God's business. You will see that the circumstances in the thoughts above are outside the control of human beings and is thus God's business.

If we do not waste our energy in minding other people's business or God's business, we can be much more focused on minding our own business, and thus be relatively stress free.

Examples of staying in "My business"

Loving myself
Taking care of my health
Maintaining peace in my mind
Doing what is right for my heart
Giving my 100% in whatever I take up
Taking full responsibility for my life without resorting to blame

This email had a powerful impact on me as I realized that a lot of my thinking and fears were based on variables that were out of my control and frankly, none of my business. Yet many of us live miserable existences because we are stuck in a loop of responsibilies that don't even belong to us. But more than that, we live attached to people's words, outcomes, and circumstances. If we just allowed God to drive and trust that he knows the way, we would be far more likely to reach our destinations with ease and without losing our bearings.

Your Signature

> Always do right. This will gratify some people and astonish the rest.
>
> —Mark Twain
> (American writer and humorist)

What You Say and What You Do Says a Lot about You

Every time we sign our name, we tell the world, "Here is my mark, my approval, my stamp, my authentication—the essence of me." In today's world, it binds us contractually, and the consequences of falsifying our signature or not following through on our contractual obligations are legally damning. In the same way, every time we walk out the door, walk into a room, face the world, or interact with others, we leave our signature too. But the signature that shows people who we are is infinitely more important than the pen-to-paper variety.

The signature of who you are not only reflects who you are as a person, but also the deeper values that you possess related to love, truth, peace, right conduct, and nonviolence. The signature people possess today is a reflection of both the outer and inner aspects of each individual. But more often than not, our signatures transcend mere words and appearances. Our signature is easily read by how we present ourselves, facial expressions, and the energy we give off. In fact, research has shown that it can take up to six months of constant interaction to change an incorrect first impression (Woods, 2013).

At the beginning of my 8th grade year, my mother was in the middle of a divorce from her second husband and I went to live with her in another city. As a result, I had to start another school. Before I could take my new seat, several of the kids came up to me to warn me about a girl named Elizabeth. She sat in the back of the class by herself. As luck would have it, the only empty seat (and my new desk) was next to hers. I was only twelve years old and I still remember this girl as if it were yesterday. She had the most disgusting habits I have ever (to this day) seen in a child. She seemed nice enough, but it was hard to get past her behavior which left a lasting impression on me as well as (I'm sure) others. And although this is a silly childhood example, it is a testament to how important it is to take care with how you present yourself to the world (or your 8th grade class).

As it goes with children, they are usually far more fixated on what is happening on the outside and less concerned about how nice a person is or their positive inner characteristics. Yet the most lasting signature comes through with how we have made someone feel. How people feel because of our presence, actions, words, and deeds are powerful reflections of our true innermost self (our values).

I would suggest, for the most part, many of the people we meet throughout the day leave us with a neutral feeling. But it is easier to recall someone who has invoked good or conversely negative emotions. The essence of our signature can be summed up in the poetic words of Maya Angelou, "At the end of the day people won't remember what you said or did, they will remember how you made them feel."

> Silver and gold are not the only coin; virtue too passes current all over the world.
>
> —(Euripides, ancient Greek poet)

So What Does Your Signature Say about You Now?

When I have taught human values to children, I would show them several different pictures and ask them to comment on each one. For the first picture, I would ask, "If you saw this pretty woman walking down the street in this full-length fur coat, what would you think about her?" Many children responded that she must be rich, famous, or important. Those few who delved in a bit deeper said that she did not have respect for animals or the planet related to the fact that she was wearing a fur coat.

But it didn't matter what they said because as you can see from this example, there are clearly different perspectives, depending upon who you ask any question. And the answer typically comes from their personal value structure. Nevertheless, correct or incorrect about their assessment of the woman, the end was the same—the woman in the picture left an impression (her signature). We all have a first impression of everyone we encounter. And as most of us know, it may be the only chance that we get to leave an imprint of who we are on someone we meet. So the questions is, "How do you want people to remember you?"

> If you hear that someone is speaking ill of you, instead of trying to defend yourself you should say: He obviously doesn't know me very well, since there are many other faults he could have mentioned.
>
> —(Epictetus, philosopher)

I love the above quote as it makes light of the fact that we all have some issue that we are dealing with in our lives. But more than that, those issues aren't for anyone to judge (including ourselves). Another great quote that I have heard is this: "What you think of me is none of my business."These are brilliant in theory and it is how we should all approach external judgement. But the quotes don't reflect the reality of how the world scrutinizes, analyzes, or evaluates people, all within a mere 100 milliseconds.

I have personally struggled with first impressions for a good portion of my adult life. As a woman who came from a very damaged childhood, I have had to deal with and work through a lot of trust issues. To mask my insecurities and shyness, I accidently created a great (or as the case may be, not so great) façade. I tried to pass off my insecurities as confidence. That approach typically backfired as most people misread the way that I carried myself as aloof and unfriendly. I was rarely able to carry off anything that even remotely resembled genuine, friendly self-assuredness. As such, my first impressions were usually described as cold and unapproachable. I have even had people tell me that at first pass, they thought I was a…*gulp*…wait for it…a b-i-t-c-h. Yes, that description always seemed to punch me right in the stomach and knock the wind out of me. I have really worked to break old patterns and be more open and approachable. This hasn't been easy as people were likened to the newspaper that the owner used to punish and beat the dog. I saw one and cringed. But as I have also learned, you can teach an old dog new tricks.

> To begin with, our perception of the world is deformed, incomplete. Then our memory is selective.
>
> —(Claude Simon, French novelist and Nobel laureate)

Now I realize that on occasion, I may regress to some old patterns. So from time to time, people still tell me that I have "presence" about me. I am guessing (or wishfully hoping) that means that I don't look outright cold anymore. I am supposing that means at times my "impression thermometer" reads lukewarm. To this day, I am sure that there are people on the planet who are still convinced in negative terms of who I am based on an interaction we had at some juncture. However, there isn't anything I can do about that except work on being the best me every day forward and not buy into other people's opinions. We all have faults as we are all human. This is where I have to revert back to the quotes with which we started. The only job we have is to play our role and remember that our words and actions as well as our outer presentation play a very big part in what the world thinks about us. But the real question is, "Do you like yourself and what you present to the world? And, would you like youself if you met yourself?" Embracing the values keeps the task of being a better version of who you are easy and authentic.

> Life is like a mirror, we get the best results when we smile at it.
>
> —(Anonymous)

Love Apples

To help combat my own issues with first impressions, many years back, I went to see a presentation coach who taught me one simple trick for my overly (and not in a good way) expressive face. "If nothing else," she said, "just try to look pleasant." I'm still not sure if she said that because she was losing faith in my ability to transform or it was sage advice that she gave everyone. But either way, she explained to me that our faces should always have what she called love apples on them. That simply meant you should have enough of a pleasant look on your face that you have rounded, high cheeks and the corners of your mouth are headed north. Ironically, by making a concerted effort to do that, it eventually led me to a more natural inclination to smile.

This was great advice on a more measurable scale as research has proven that there is something in psychology called an emotional contagion. In essence, this theory states that the way we feel is considered contagious. So whatever we are feeling, whether it is joy or frustration, it can impact those around us. Since I had what seemed to be a perpetually unpleasant look on my face, my coach was merely trying to teach me to "fake it until I make it." Essentially, she wanted me to infect myself with my own smile until I was able to change my state of being. She was on to something as there is a lot more to this smiling theory.

According to Dr. Mark Stibich, smiling does the following:

1. Boosts the immune system
2. Increases positive effect
3. Reduces stress
4. Lowers blood pressure
5. Enhances other people's perception of you

Let me save you the hundreds of dollars I spent to get this information. The simple point in all of this is that a smile can go a long way. And it makes a great first impression. For some people, smiling is as natural as blinking their eyes. For others, it might take a crowbar to turn their frown upside down. Making a genuine effort to smile and be pleasant is a powerful and positive way to impact those around you. When is the last time you smiled and meant it?

> If we get our self-esteem from superficial places, from our popularity, appearance, business success, financial situation, health, any of these, we will be disappointed, because no one can guarantee that we'll have them tomorrow.
>
> —(Kathy Ireland, American model and actress)

Judging the Book by Its Cover

Most of the world has become lost in the outer signature. In the United States alone, the cosmetics industry brings in approximately ten billion dollars a year. Depending upon which website you look at, the total worldwide spending is estimated between $30 and $44 billion dollars. That said, it is clear that the focus of external beauty is not limited to the Western world, but the USA certainly has a strong market share.

For example, in certain Asian countries, there has been an increase in eyelid, complete face restructuring, and rhinoplasty surgeries. The latest trend is calf reductions to make the legs look stick thin. Even in the Middle East where vanity is supposed to be limited, there is an excess of "plastic women" wandering the streets of places like Lebanon, the United Arab Emirates, etc. The newest craze there seems to be injecting fat or fillers into the face, leaving the women with excessively large-looking cheeks, overly taut skin, and with what I call the lion lady look. These trends have become so prevalent and (in some cases) extreme that I came across an article where a Chinese man was suing his wife for having ugly children. He found out that she had completely altered her looks to the point where she did not even remotely resemble the woman in her "before" pictures.

Nowadays, the way we look, dress, and present ourselves tend to supersede any viable, valuable, or important internal characteristics that we possess. This is why some people focus obsessively and use their outer appearance to mask the ugliness (sadness, insecurity, depression, etc.) that they have inside. We have become a society of people thinking, "I'm not good enough." This idea is perpetuated in a world where more often than not, who we are tends to be fundamentally unimportant until we can prove ourselves as somehow desirable on the outside.

I can't speak for any other woman, but most days, I feel like I am judged from the roots of my hair to the heels of my shoes. But I'd venture to guess that we've all been on the giving or receiving end of judgment. We've spent time wondering what's real or not. We look at someone else's clothes, hair, makeup, facial expressions and body language as an assessment of their personal and/or financial value. From that point, we may categorize them as worthy or not to move forward on a more personal level. More often than not, many of us make a solid decision about the course of our relationship within mere seconds of meeting someone without any viable dialog. In an effort to make the decision process a bit quicker, I have often thought about making cute little notes to paste to myself, stating all the effort and/or money I spent to "pull myself together" that day. I mean, if you knew right away that my hair was done by Michael Canale or Supercuts, wearing a Victoria's Secret or Walmart bra and an Armani or Kmart dress, could we more quickly brush past external formalities and move to a place of depth and meaning?

It's not just the personal insecurities and some random public scrutiny that we have to deal with on a day-to-day basis. There are some real biases in our world about the way people look. Research has proven this theory time and again, showing that attractive people are more likely to secure better positions in the workforce and even make more money. Good-looking people are more likely to receive assistance or help from strangers. Even scientists have proven that babies are more interested in good-looking faces. Based on that simple fact, it seems that we humans are hardwired to focus on the external. As such, it appears there is no denying that human beings have a natural propensity toward beauty. This isn't a bad thing. But where do we draw the line and find value in people, not designer labels? What people fail to remember is that although beauty is an initial attractor, so is confidence and genuine warmth. However, the latter of the two will remain with you forever.

> "Everything has its beauty, but not everyone sees it."
>
> —(Confucius, teacher, editor, politician, and philosopher from Chinese history)

What You See Is not Always What You Get

In 2007, I married a beautiful Spaniard that I met in a café while living in Madrid. We married only a few months after we met. We did this for two reasons: (1) we needed residency papers to stay together, and (2) we were both broken souls in search of certainty and love and completely inept at meeting our needs in a healthy manner.

I knew to the core of my being that we should not have gotten married. We didn't know each other well enough, and our "love" was just a desperate, clinging need to fulfill what was missing in both of our lives due to tumultuous upbringings. One year after we married, we separated. I went back to Korea for the second time to teach English, and he moved to the Baleares on the island of Ibiza. Our two years together were, at best, horrendous. But we tried in our own limited ways to mend something that was never together in the first place. In a last-ditch effort to save my marriage, I moved to Ibiza at the end of my teaching contract in 2009. I arrived in Ibiza on February 15, and by May 1, I left him as the last straw was that he had cheated on me with zero remorse for his actions. Once again, I was betrayed by someone proclaiming to love me. Another event to strengthen my excuse not to trust.

I decided to stay in Ibiza as I loved the island and had made some wonderful friends. However, I was desperately in need of money. So I had to take a job as a hostess on a twenty-seven-meter yacht. My ego was mortified that it was serving people with all its education. In my head, someone was supposed to be giving me fresh towels and an appletini as I lounged on the starboard deck, cruising over the Mediterranean or docking off the island of Formentera. So when the yacht guests would ask me, "How long have you been doing this?" I sharply responded that I had a PhD and was trying to raise money to fund my writing. However, the real truth was that I was a PhD who was going through a painful divorce, living on an island that I could not afford. It was humbling, but I needed to do what I had to do. Plus, as I have come to learn, the universe always gives us what we need when we need it. Interestingly, what I learned (and needed) that summer was more valuable than any spiritual advancement class I could have ever taken or the money I earned.

> Judgments prevent us from seeing the good that lies beyond appearances.
>
> —(Wayne Dyer, American self-help author and speaker)

The Man I'll Call Mark

When the owners of the yacht weren't using it, it was rented out to wealthy tourists. One day, an extremely overweight (but not completely unfortunate) man (who we'll call Mark) came onto the boat with his new blond, thin, gorgeous wife and her two children. Immediately, my mind went into judgment mode. How could such a beautiful woman be with such a heavy, average-looking man? Clearly, she was only with him because of his money.

As it turned out, Mark and his family spent a lot of time with us that summer. It wasn't until after I had gotten to know him that I saw past his exterior features. What I came to realize was that Mark was one of the warmest, patient, loving, funny, generous human beings I had ever met. He was absolutely amazing. I could clearly see why his wife chose to marry him. He was a wonderful human being that exuded far more radiance and love than what he could ever have presented on his exterior.

Since meeting that couple, I have made a concerted effort to try my hardest to see people beyond what is on the outside. This isn't an easy task as we all have a clear list of our preferences as well as what defines what we are looking for from a friend, partner, boss, etc.

The problem I had is that I was bogged down by that list and was attracting the same dysfunctional people recycled in different packages. That summer, I learned to keep an open mind and toss out any antiquated beliefs that I held about perfection. I began to wonder how many diamonds I had disregarded as dirty coal. From that day, I vowed I would never again want to miss out on the precious jewels that come in deceiving packages—like Mark.

> If you judge people, you have no time to love them.
>
> —(Mother Teresa, Catholic nun, humanitarian)

Realistically Speaking

Granted, there isn't anything wrong with having an eye for beauty or detail. Putting yourself together and having respect for who you are and the way you present yourself can be very positive. We should also eat right, exercise, bathe regularly, etc. As a matter of fact, it is the value defined as right conduct to take care of the vehicle we define as the body. It is part of our signature that says, "I take care of myself. I love myself. I feel good about myself." But taken out of proportion or context, it can also say, "I am shallow and superficial," "I only care about myself," "I am insecure and unhappy," or "I don't feel worthy of love the way I am," "I need to fix myself." As such, there can be (and usually is) a fine line regarding what our outer signature is really saying about us and who we truly are. Typically, the more we do to repair or improve the outside, the more confusion, chaos, or unhappiness resides on the inside. So it is important to bring forth a healthy balance of emotional well-being, health, and fitness as well as the other external variables.

We can't (and shouldn't) rest on our laurels on what we look like. Too many people in our society do that, and it only perpetuates the desire to only want to be qualities based upon what we are on the outside. We need to find a space of love and acceptance for who we are without Botox, fillers, or surgery. We need to be more than what is on the outside. We need to love people for their virtues, not for their Versace.

But sadly, the "more" seems to have gotten us lost in the depths of ego-centered identity. We are emotionally void, trying to fill the hole with creams, pills, and procedures. Our hearts are screaming, "I'm not enough if I am not thin/beautiful/smart/cellulite-free/etc.!" But this is not true. Botox or not, you *are* enough—cellulite or not, you are enough; eye lift or not, you are enough; rich or not, you are enough! Repeat after me, "I am enough just the way I am!"

Yet more often than not, we are only judging the book by its cover (as I did with Mark) and potentially missing out on some really great stories. (This includes our own fabulous story because we are so busy judging ourselves.) In the end, in the simplest of terms, we are destroying our children, us, and our world by not focusing on our own or other's innate goodness or the concepts that are truly important—values, morals, and ethics.

> There's always a lot to be thankful for if you take time to look for it. For example, I am sitting here thinking how nice it is that wrinkles don't hurt.
>
> —(Author unknown)

The Aging Epidemic

I know all too well about the topic of aging. Once I stepped into my forties, I became obnoxiously aware of every fine line, sag, or gray hair that popped up. I think once you hit your forties, aging is like an epidemic of the chicken pox: it starts with one spot (or wrinkle), and then all of a sudden, you seem to be covered! To make my obsession worse, at the time, I was living abroad in Seoul, Korea, where people sought out perfection to an almost grotesque and dangerous degree. (Although I am going to give credit where it is due, Korean plastic surgeons are masterful artists. If I ever did feel that need to head down that road, it would be a Korean doctor performing the work.) I could not move through my day without seeing a cosmetic surgery advertisement where someone was shown completely transformed to an upgraded, almost unrecognizable version of themselves. Constantly seeing this, I became obsessed and somewhat possessed with the whole concept of fixing myself. I was like a cosmetic procedure, zombie-walking around with no awareness, repeating in a droned-out voice, "Fillers, lifting, peels." I wanted to have it all done. I had an insatiable appetite to know what was out there and available to cure my aging problem.

I would visit any doctor who would give me a free consultation, just to hear how he or she could turn back the hands of time and restore me to the youth of my long-lost twenties. It was such a relief to hear that I was not doomed to look like this forever. Moreover, the good news was that most of my problems could be eradicated (short-term) for a small fee, a dose of Botulinum toxin (a.k.a. Botox), and 1cc of Juvéderm. There were two things that stopped that process from happening. I'd like to think that the first one was good sense. But the truth is that fortunately, it was also a time where I was relatively broke, or I might have left that country looking like some others who have dabbled a bit too far in excessive reconstruction that hasn't gone well. I won't mention any names. But we all know of a few people whose doctors should have said no or at least no more.

I am still not completely cured of my fixation. I have to catch myself more often than I care to admit assessing the situation in the mirror and imagining how one of the many treatments available could easily sort out the problem. I still buy vials of hope disguised as the latest miracle cream. My mind is not ready to give up my fixation quite yet. But I have come to understand a more important lesson. What I realize (and what tends to supersede most of my desires) is that when

I am fixating on my perceived imperfections, coming back to the values helps curb my appetite for a lot of things that could potentially get out of hand.

It is simply about all of us realizing and genuinely feeling that we are enough and perfect just the way we are—wrinkles, cellulite, and all. We all have talents and gifts that far supersede any external variable. It is about opening our hearts to ourselves just the way we are and as God made us—perfect. This is where we should hold our value. This is where we start to believe that we are whole and good enough. This is where our divinity lies. It is the seat of our soul. It is the gift that God has given us. It is more than what we look like. It is who we are, what we believe, how we act, and what we are giving back to the world that truly defines our real beauty.

In my lifetime, I have seen a lot of gorgeous women who were extremely ugly people. Conversely, I have seen some unattractive people who absolutely radiated love and beauty. Which would you rather be?

> If wealth is lost, nothing is lost.
> If health is lost, something is lost.
> If character is lost, everything is lost.
>
> —(Chinese proverb)

Why Do We Need Values?

We need only to look around the world, and we will see an abundance of crime, bullying, substance abuse, violence against others and the planet, and an overall decline in the morality of our society and leadership to understand why these values are so important to the success of our personal, spiritual, and planetary evolution.

When I first returned to the States, I moved to the East Bay/Oakland area of California. One day, I was taking my dogs for their daily walk, and there was a young girl walking in front of me on the sidewalk. She could not have been much more than eleven or twelve. She knew that I was behind her. As we were walking, she kept picking up trash and throwing it behind her in an attempt to hit me and my dogs. I suppose she thought she was being funny (or just flat-out malicious). I finally caught up to her and scolded her for not taking care that she could injure someone, but also pointed out that she was littering. At that point, she just gave me a smirk and an inappropriate gesture. I went home completely convinced that the upcoming generation was going to be a bunch of sociopaths. I know this is not true. There is no such thing as a bad person, just bad behavior. However, children are in desperate need of these values as their foundation. But if adults don't have their heads set on straight and live by a strong moral code, how will children learn what is correct behavior? This young girl was more than likely mimicking what she had been exposed to in one form or another. Although she was making the choice to throw the trash, her moral structure was set into place long ago by some external variables that enforced that kind of conduct. That is just one incident that clearly reinforced the idea that values need to be the cornerstone of our lives and educational system—not test scores.

Without values, we become morally bankrupt. The Indian spiritual leader Sathya Sai Baba once said, "Good and evil are present in the mind of man, not in the world." The problems of the world won't go away by trying to fix them on the outside. We can point fingers and place blame until the moon rises and the sun sets. But it isn't going to change the way things are in the world. Transformation will only occur when we take responsibility and work on ourselves from within—when we embrace and live our lives through human values.

It's kind of like my wrinkles. I could have done something drastic externally to fix them. But in the end, it wouldn't resolve the underlying issue, which was that I didn't fully love and accept myself as I was. So thinking that we can change our circumstances by moving, changing partners, jobs, avoiding responsibility, going to war, surgery, etc., are all very temporary fixes to where the real problems lie—inside us. That may be a hard pill to swallow for some people. But the fact is that all of our problems are really (in some way) our own doing.

> We can't solve problems by using the same kinds of thinking we used when we created them.
>
> —(Albert Einstein, physicist)

Life: The Great Big Mirror

Most New Age spiritual practices teach us that our outer world is merely a reflection and reaction of our inner world. In other words, our own thoughts and feelings create what we perceive as going on around us. So in fact, the thoughts you think and what you perceive end up being your choice. This school of thought suggests that the only way to change what's going on around you is to change what's going on within you. So theoretically, if you only change your thoughts, feelings, reactions, or inner turmoil, the problem will go away. This seems like incredibly simplistic thinking. It is also a process that doesn't work without some key elements. The first thing is that we need to have conscious awreness that we are even having recurring thougths that are not in our highest good. From there, we need to figure out how to stop the cyclical thoughts patterns. Often times, saying (aloud or in our head) a word like "Stop" or "cancel" work to redirect our focus. With enough practice, it becomes relatively easy to stop thoughts, but remaining aware of our thoughts is a bit more challenging as we often unconsciously get trapped in our loops. The last component to successfully changing our inner dialog is that we really need to believe what we are thinking. So although we can stop thoughts and shift them into another direction, we must really believe to our core that what we say is our truth. This is the piece that a lot of people miss when they use the laws of attraction. If you continue to think that your bank account will grow, but believe to your core that you aren't worthy of being financially secure, it won't happen for you. What makes this process even more challenging is that often times, we have core beliefs that have settled into us at a cellular level. Once that happens, they are a bit harder to eradicate. But when you are working to be better and incorporate the values, life will give you plenty of mirrors to look into to help you along the path of righteousness.

Mirror, Mirror on the Wall

As an example, for the most part, I can say that I typically get on well with most people. I can also easily say that there are very few people that I have disliked throughout my life. Moreover, if I do find that I have an aversion toward someone, it is usually a short-term problem. However, during my last year abroad in Korea, I had a supervisor who triggered a horrible reaction every time I saw her or we spoke. She was the head teacher of the English Department. To me, she was unprofessional, unkind, with no understanding of what she was supposed to be doing. She never seemed to smile. Plus, she didn't have some important skills that I felt she needed to effectively do her job. She made me downright furious.

I can't remember ever having such a strong reaction about any one single person in my whole life. But with this woman, I would obsess about how I was going to tell her off, embarrass, and expose her for her lack of knowledge. There was a stalker in my head, and she wasn't relenting. This went on for almost ten months. It could have gone on longer, but thankfully, I gained control of my values. But it wasn't really until the end of my contract that I could finally see her as the person that she was because I had begun to open my heart to her.

I came to find out that there was a lot of stress and unhappiness in her life, coupled with fear. She was under a lot of pressure from the principal, who had given her an overload of responsibilities. She was a mother of two young boys, and she was having challenges in her marriage. She later also told me that she had never met anyone like me, and she felt intimidated by my presence. She also felt shame that she could not speak better English. She was shy and avoided trying to communicate with me. When I looked back at the situation objectively, I can now see that she also represented things that I did not like or allow within myself. Not only did she represent my insecurities, but she also reflected my fears. And the more I focused on my negative energy and anger toward her, the more closed I became to seeing her with my heart. But I didn't just close off my heart to her; I had closed the door to connecting with myself.

Believe It or Not, It's Just Me

As I mentioned, in the past, I had a real issue with maintaining a pleasant look on my face. I have also been very hard on myself to be perfect and professional. I insisted on doing a good job. As a matter of fact, I defined myself by the outcome. This theoretically, in some ways, would seem positive, but it's not—at least not all the time. Sometimes, it is just another aspect of having power and control issues or low self-worth. Moreover, it stopped me from doing a lot of things. If I thought I could not do something right the first time, I didn't attempt it at all. I had to maintain my façade of perfection at all costs. As a result, I became very shy and somewhat reclusive. It also resulted in the inability to not allow myself to be vulnerable. To me, vulnerability equated to weakness. And for the most part, as I highlighted earlier, I picked myself apart, flaw by tiny flaw. I was in a losing emotional battle with myself.

All the nitpicking and judgment were certainly not kind ways to treat anyone, much less myself. So as it turned out, all the things that I seemingly abhorred about my coworker were a reflection of what I was struggling within myself. I really needed to see these issues to work on them. At the time, I could not see these problematic aspects within myself. As such, my co-worker was a massive mirror image that relentlessly and annoyingly vied for my attention. Because I didn't want to look at myself, I became angry. The situation was a great test to see if I would use my values or yield to my ego. For some time, the score board had an unequal amount of ticks in favor of my ego. But in the end, I am proud to report the values won out.

In truth, I am not sure that some of the realizations I eventually had about her would have made much difference as early on I needed to work through the issues within myself to release her with love. That took some time. But this is an example of how we can't get what we can't give. I wanted something from her that I could not give (or be) myself. In addition, it is a gentle reminder that when we hate or dislike people, it isn't so much about what they've done. It is really about what they represent or reflect back to us. The good news about all of this is that once your value structure is firmly rooted, you will be able to move more freely and harmoniously throughout the world as these good principles will be the reflections and reactions you start to see and experience in your life.

> The unexamined life is not worth living.
> —(Socrates, Greek-Athenian philosopher)

Why These Specific Values?

These are the five straightforward, inherent human values that lie within each and every one of us: love, peace, truth, right conduct, and nonviolence. They are the basis of religious doctrines and spiritual principles. They are at the core of morality. They are our very nature. And although these words may seem retro, hippish, or even rudimentary, they are and will forever be the cornerstone of our survival as human beings. We can't successfully function as good, peaceful, honest, loving, morally-based humans without these values any more than we can survive without air. These values must not only be examined and understood at a fundamental level, but fully integrated into our beings and passed down to our children.

What we say and what we do are really who we are at the very essence of our being. Our words and (more importantly) our actions are the authentic signatures that we all impart on this world. As an extreme example, it doesn't work to preach nonviolence and then go join the military any more than you can claim to be a vegetarian and eat meat. These inconsistencies and double messages are what leave an everlasting mark on strangers, family, friends, and the entire world around us.

This rule also applies to what we teach our children. For example, if you want your children to speak quietly, it won't help to scream at them. In the same way, it would not make sense to strike your child for hitting. Each and every day, we need to remember to walk our talk. When you can do this, you will feel better about yourself. And the contentment you find by being living proof of your truth will radiate out to those around you.

Where Do We Start?

We start by wanting to change and work toward being the best and most complete version of ourselves. Then, we assess where we've been and where we'd like to go from this moment forward. Once we take full responsibility for our lives, choices, mistakes, and successes, we take a deep breath and say, "Today is the first day of the rest of my life." And ask yourself how you want the story to continue? From there, we go back to the basics (love, truth, peace, right conduct, and nonviolence). We live, eat, breathe, and imbibe these values. And when we falter, we get back up and start again until they are wholly integrated into every fiber of our being. This suggestion may seem extreme or even radical to some, but it is not impossible. As Charles W. Chesnutt once said, "Impossibilities are merely things of which we have not learned, or which we do not wish to happen."

Love

True and Selfless Love manifests as sacrifice. Such love knows no hatred. It envelops the entire universe, and is capable of drawing near even those who are seemingly far away. In the phenomenal world, you come across many shades and derivatives of this primordial love. You love your father, mother, brother, sister, spouse, friends and others. In all such cases, there is always a tinge of selfishness somewhere or the other. Divine love, on the other hand, is totally free of even the slightest trace of selfishness. You must surrender to such love, become completely submerged by it, and experience the bliss it confers. True and Selfless Love manifests itself as sacrifice. For acquiring Divine love, the quality of Kshama (forbearance and patience) is a vital necessity. Every individual must cultivate this noble quality.

—Divine Discourse, May 25, 2000.

Love (Prema)

> It is pure love that bestows liberation. You should endeavor to attain this holistic love. To attain liberation, people should undertake all sorts of spiritual practices, but love is the undercurrent of all spiritual endeavors.
>
> —Sathya Sai Baba (Indian guru, spiritual figure, and educator)

What Is the Value of Love?

Love is the most important of the five human values. It is the value that sets the foundation for all the other values. Love is absolutely critical on the journey toward incorporating the values into your life. Without it, there can only be fleeting success with all the other values.

When we are asked where to find love in our bodies, we point to our hearts. This is the seat of love. It is where we feel love in its purest form. It is what we all strive for in our evolutionary journey. Our entire purpose on this planet is to love and be loved. Love is the quickest pathway to God (and your God self), embracing your divine potential and living in bliss. Love as a value is the cornerstone, the seed, the beginning, the gateway to all the other values. If you lived with complete love for everything and everyone, every other value would naturally come into alignment. If you lived completely in love, you'd never hold a grudge, feel pain, or confusion. You wouldn't be able to because true love is pure. It is God. The concept of love is so uncomplicated yet conversely a word and idea that have become terribly distorted in its definition. However, love cannot be judged or measured. It is only felt. Thoughts of love must be followed by words of kindness and acts of selflessness, or else love becomes meaningless (Dewan, 2003).

Because of media and other random variables in our lives, typically, many view love as a romantic notion that is supposed to conjure up warm, fuzzy feelings and bring about a notion of "happily ever after." Some even go so far as to describe this feeling as "butterflies in their stomach." I have also heard love described as the "it" factor. It has similarly been defined as a significant other that "makes you happy." When people aren't defining love, there is a large majority of those who always seem to be on a perpetual quest to find it. We listen to songs about love. We read books about love. We watch movies about love. However, none of what we have romanticized love to be is really love. It is the little girl's story book where the prince comes to save the princess and all ends well. It is the Hollywood version of love used to sell tickets at the box office. But neither of those or the meanings we've come to associate with the concept are entirely accurate. Love is actually rather simple. In its purest form, it is (1) unconditional, and (2) love in action, which is service to others. What love is *not* is selfish, punitive, painful, or being rescued by a man on a horse.

Everyone Has His Opinion

Love is interconnectedness to everyone and everything. It is not thinking and processing. It is being in a constant state of love, which comes from your heart center, not your mind. However, all of us have at one time or another tried to compartmentalize love. Love is not restrictive or judgmental. It is not granted to some and denied to others. You can't put love in a box or mark it with a label because it is all-encompassing. It is the box. It is the label, and it is all the space in between. It is everything. Yet as I moved around the world, no matter where I have been or what culture I lived in, I found that we all tend to want to make love fit into our lives as a means to justify feelings and actions. We say that we want love. Some of us even pronounce to love deeply. Our false sense of love holds out and proclaims, "I will do anything for love." But then there is a caveat as it finishes, by announcing, "But I won't do that" (Meatloaf song lyrics).

Love is an intensely powerful force. It has the capability to overcome any obstacle. It is also one of the hardest concepts to practice as it takes purity and unconditional regard for everyone. As I was on a personal quest to understand love, I wanted to get a better sense of what it meant to love. I wanted to hear how people defined love and their thoughts related to love. So I started talking to people from around the world about their ideas surrounding the concept.

One of the first conversations I recall came more as a forced accident than as an actual planned inquiry.

The conversation was with a married man living in the United Arab Emirates. His marriage had been on the rocks for years. Their relationship was like a roller coaster that tended to continually plummet to a dark, shadowy, abusive end and then temporarily rise to a truce. After moving there, I met him through the school where I worked. We got to know each other better after I volunteered to help a group put together a free concert. We were also both part of the same yoga group. Since I was new in town, he introduced me to his wife and children as well as an assortment of other lovely people.

During that time, I didn't have a car, so he would generously swing by my house and taxi me to our weekly yoga session. This man had a big heart and went out of his way to help and support people in need. However, because (unbeknownst to me) there were already festering issues in his marriage, his wife decided to sorely misdirect her insecurities and anger and accused us of having an affair. With my human values in place, I did what I could to stay out of their problems and not engage in or feed the drama. But their problems only escalated, and she was crying out to have her needs met at the expense of an innocent bystander—me. Moreover, it isn't good form to accuse a woman of having an unsubstantiated affair with a married man when you live in the Middle East. In fact, it is dangerous.

But with my values in focus, I could remain somewhat objective as it was clear her pain was deeper than I could ever begin to imagine. Moreover, engaging in the drama by trying to defend my honor would only exacerbate an already-volatile situation. Not engaging in the energy released any part I was playing much more quickly as I did not give any reason to add further attention to my being. My only part to play was to send her love and release her with love. Love allowed me to honor her journey.

After all the intense marital discord between him and his wife, I became curious about the dynamic between them. I was confused as to why they would stay together only to abuse, manipulate, and hurt each other as they were clearly not meeting each other's needs in a healthy manner. From what I could see, love was clearly not the cornerstone of their relationship. So I asked him about his views regarding love to try to gain some understanding regarding their situation. He tried desperately to convince me that there are several forms of love. He rationalized the abuse and conflict in his relationship by using the Indian concepts of *sattvic* (pure and good), *rajistic* (passionate and aggressive), and *tomasic* (dull and ignorant). He claimed that love would continue to cycle through all of these phases. He also told me that his wife's actions "were simply the *love* of a jealous woman just trying to protect her man." In his mind, he was justifying her actions as healthy and loving behavior.

As I listened to his rationale, I realized two important things. The first was that we humans create definitions for love to suit our needs. In his case, he was trying to sell me on the fact that the possessiveness and violence in his marriage were forms of love. All I could think (what would logically come to most people's mind) were the words "abusive and controlling," but certainly nothing that would relate to love, only a lack of love and a rise of the ego. The second was that the words he was using were not related to love but were "stages" (if you will) that many people go through in relationships because we are using our false self (ego) to navigate through our definition of love. Along with these stages, we also have our human emotions highlighted with the ego's overwhelming desire to be superior. Beyond that, at no point is abuse (verbal or physical) to be defined as love. Hurting someone you profess to care for is selfish and violent. So, when you put all these variables together, you don't get love. You get justification for feelings and actions that you have within a dynamic called a relationship. You can't get love from mixing these elements together any more than you can make a sweet cake from old milk and fish.

> When the power of love overcomes the love of power, the world will know peace.
>
> —(Jimi Hendrix, musician)

One night over wine and cheese while sitting at my little kitchen table in Madrid, I was talking to a young American woman who had been divorced. We were both talking about failed relationships and dissecting where they go wrong. We agreed that a lack of communication and love were the two primary issues surrounding unsuccessful interactions with people in our lives. After some time, I started telling her about a friend of mine who had a wonderful marriage where the communication was open and honest. In all the time they had been married, they had never had a fight. The way they would address an issue was simple. They would sit down as two rational adults and discuss their problem over tea, finding a way to compromise and/or work through their challenges. After telling her about this relationship, the young woman quickly said, "That's not normal. You need to fight if you love each other." I was taken aback by her statement and countered it with a question. I asked her, "Does it sound accurate to you that anger, ego, and 'my right is more right' could be the correct definition of 'normal,' much less love?" Although this wasn't the first time I had heard this rationale, I was reminded of the distorted connection between the human mind and the purity of love. That night before I slept, I could not help but wonder how we got to the place in our evolution where we could reasonably use the concepts of love and anger interchangeably.

Arguing Isn't the Problem; Your Ego Is

Of course, just because you argue with your partner, it doesn't mean that you can't find and return to a place where you hold a space for love and understanding. Usually, discord is the psyche crying out to have its needs met. It is disconnecting from your heart and moving to your head. The fact of the matter is that relationships can be the quickest way to spiritual development. The challenge is navigating the rough terrain that can come about in your relationships. But there are tricks to doing this. And it doesn't mean caving in or becoming a martyr. It means open dialog. It not tanking feelings and letting them build to a boiling point. It means taking responsibility for you part in the discord. It means talking in a loving tone and not place blame before you have all facts at your disposal. As Joseph Joubert once said, "The aim of argument, or of discussion, should not be victory, but progress."

It is also important to keep in that argument is nothing more than the rise of the ego. It's the ego's way of fighting for its position and feeding the endless hunger that it has and needs for survival. It is the belief that you are separate from your beloved, boss, friend, etc. But you are not; we are all one. We are all love, and that cosmic energy has the power to heal and eradicate any discord *if* you move back to purity of love. These "incidents" can also lead to great personal and spiritual growth if we can look at the situation objectively and realize that it is not love that is guiding us in a heated discussion. It is the ego's desire to be right at all costs and have its needs met. It is also about feeling you are not safe, missing out on something, and/or allowing a fear to take over.

> The direction of the mind is more important than its progress.
>
> —(Joseph Joubert, French moralist and essayist)

At the core of a heated battle, most people really just want to feel safe and be loved. Whether most people want to admit it or not, nearly everyone on the planet is looking for two things out of life: security and unconditional love. As I mentioned before, our real life purpose is to love and be loved. It has even been suggested that God created man to have someone to love Him. Since love is the destination we are all trying to head toward, it just becomes petty and sad when we let our egos override our true heart's desire and then justify our negative behaviors as love. Relationships are one of the best ways that we can put ourselves on the fast track to practice this and other values. But we need to have more conscious awareness as we move through our lives. Sadly, people are stuck in old, outdated ideas about how loving relationships work. We are also more willing to give up when things don't go as we plan or there is the slightest bit of discord.

But there is the thing, when our ego is not fighting for its position in a relationship, research has shown us that love for another can actually have exceptional healing properties. Not only does it increase our feel-good hormones, but we also have a decrease in stress, and our blood pressure may decrease slightly. People in loving relationships are said to live longer too. In fact, the Huffington Post (2012) reported on love's impact on us: "In one of the studies, researchers looked at 34 couples who lived together and tested for the stress hormone cortisol before, during and after being separated for four to seven days. Researchers found that when the couples were separated physically, they had higher cortisol levels and had worse sleep than when they were together."

Love is not only the cornerstone of our value structure. But it is also necessary for our health and well-being.

The Anti-Love

Many years ago, I was living in the southwest. I was visiting a friend and her new husband. The entire time I was in their home, they were bickering. I pulled my friend aside to inquire about her emotional state as she seemed terribly distressed. She told me that she was fine and that the fighting was "normal." In fact, she said, "We fight with as much passion as the love we have for each other." Again, I was stunned by her train of thought. In her mind, she associated love with passion and passion with anger. That thinking is clearly askew and illogical. One is in no way the other. This is another example of redefined love that is powered by the ego and not the heart. After some time, we lost contact with each other. But my best assumption is that the marriage may not have lasted. In the long run, it doesn't work to rationalize or identify your ego with or as love. Moreover, it isn't good for anyone's emotional health or relationship to be in a constant state of stress and emotional dissonance.

Adult relationships are not the only place that love gets lost in translation. I have heard many skewed definitions of love from parents who say things like "I work hard to give my kids everything. What more do they want?" To this I just want to shout, "They want to be heard, seen for who they are, touched, and loved unconditionally!" I understand that parents want to give their children a better life. I get that parents want to see their children happy. But, it is also important to understand that things of temporal value can never replace a hug, kiss, or a kind word. In fact, research has proven that touching is essential for the healthy development of children. Not only is it good for heart health and bonding, but one study found that, "Korean infants in an orphanage who received an extra fifteen minutes of a female voice, massage and eye-to-eye contact, five days a week for four weeks, gained more weight and had greater increases in body length and head circumferences after the four weeks and at six months of age than children without the extra stimulation" (sixwise.com). This is the power of love.

The stories I shared are associated with how the human mind relates to our current definition of love, but as you have read, something has been seriously lost in translation. We need love for our physical and emotional well-being. Love is the positive driving force behind everything that is and is to be. We can't live in this world without love. And we should never settle for anything less than perfection in our love. But more than that, there isn't an amount of money or anything in the world that can buy lasting, unconditional love. The only exchange or currency for love is love itself.

Until Death Do Us Part or Divorce, Whichever Comes First

If the examples I have provided aren't enough to give you food for thought about how people have come to mistakenly redefine love, let's look at some of the reasons why people get divorced. As you can guess, divorce is the extreme result of redefined love. According to psychpage.com, the two main reasons people get divorced are "high conflict" and "loss of intimacy and connection." Within the constructs of high conflict, money is often cited as the number one reason for divorce. (I have heard that sharing a bathroom is second.) If these are in fact the case, it would only stand to reason that trying to make a relationship about money or into a competition to win battles and make your point (ego-centered behaviors) would be in direct conflict with healthy boundaries, open communication, and anything remotely related to the concept of unconditional love; hence, divorce.

As I see relationships, the concepts of love and connection have become more about the physical manifestation of our emotional well-being. If we are in a good emotional state, we can express ourselves and love more freely. If we are in a negative emotional place, we tend to withhold love. So love becomes subject to how we feel and if we feel our needs are being met. This distorts the true essence of love and gets lost in the ego's emotive rollercoaster. Love should always be at the forefront of who we are and how we interact with others. It should not be used in a powerplay or as a tool to coherce or cajole another. It should always be given in its purest form—unconditionally.

Of course, love isn't only about marriage or significant relationships. This topic just happens to be the one point where we contractually commit to love one another. It is also one of our biggest societal failures because the idea and definition of love has become so jaded and, quite frankly, wrong. These days, divorce seems to be the quickest way to rid ourselves of our problems instead of looking for a way back to love. Before we are even married, we crack jokes that refer to our "starter husband" our "future ex-wife." We aren't even starting out dedicated to the idea of commitment much less the concept of lasting, unconditional love. We have to find a way to get back to the purity and essence of the word. If we could do that, we could seriously put a dent in the nearly 68 percent divorce rate this country is facing. Divorce isn't the answer. Love is!

A Typical Problem

A lovely young Korean woman I met during my last year in Korea told me that she was feeling a great amount of sadness in her marriage. Apparently, her husband had been telling her that she was not showing him enough love and affection. Her lack of attention toward him was causing anger and frustration. The discord between them was growing to the point where she had moved out and was seriously considering divorce. He was not only demanding love, but he was using his words to hurt her in an extreme effort to gain attention from her. He wanted to be connected to her and feel significant in their relationship, but didn't know how to approach his needs in a healthy way.

She also shared with me that her husband was a workaholic. After work, he didn't want to do anything but, as she put it, breathe. He was so focused on his work and being a success that he didn't take the time for anything else in his life, much less meeting his own basic needs. As a result, he stopped meeting her needs as well. In response, she was unable to give him what he needed because she was feeling abandoned, insecure, and unloved. The two had created quite an unhealthy dynamic.

So Whose Fault Is It?

Her husband was not nurturing or caring for himself. In addition to that, he was crying out to have some of his basic human needs met. He was just going about it the wrong way. By effectively ignoring himself and not feeding his own soul, he ended up having feelings of emptiness and longing. He was also probably avoiding long-standing issues from his past. As a result, without knowing it, he wanted his wife to give him what he was unwilling or able to give himself—love.

Yes, it is one thing to try to get back to the heart of love in a relationship, but we can't give or fill any void in another person. Only we can truly find what fills our soul and makes our heart sing. Sure, we can fill someone up and give them what they need for a while. We can be supportive, loving, etc. But no one can ever permanently fulfill what we feel is (consciously or unconsciously) missing within us. It may feel like someone can for a time, but in the end, their efforts will never be enough. Making ourselves happy and at peace and opening our heart space is part of our individual journey. It is not for someone else to do for us.

This is the biggest illusion we have when we meet someone. We start to feel excitement and a new passion for life. We believe that it is all because this new person is "making us happy." No, they aren't. They are only temporarily filling a hole that you failed to address. After some time, you may come to a place in your evolution where your needs change. When that happens, your partner's presence may become obsolete or an annoyance. This happens because they no longer fill the original void, and your sense of happiness dissipates. Oftentimes, this is or will be the demise of your relationship because very few couples go to the core of their issues to see what went wrong and devise a plan to get on to a path back to true love. That is another reason why our divorce rate is so disproportionately high in this country.

> Plant your own garden and decorate your own soul, instead of waiting for someone to bring you flowers.
>
> —(Veronica A. Shoffstall, Poet)

To start out on the journey toward a healthy relationship, we must love ourselves first. Otherwise, we get lost in the deception of what is or isn't lacking in our lives, thus creating discord in our relationships through blame, resentment, and misunderstanding.

As in the case of the woman, any effort that she was making toward her husband ended up being somewhat futile. No matter how small or large her gesture, it was or would eventually never be sufficient as her husband needed to fill the void and emptiness from within. He needed to open his heart to himself. But because he could not see that he was not caring for himself, he laid all the responsibility on her. As such, her love "was not enough." Now, I am not suggesting that she didn't have a part to play as I am a firm believer that it takes two to make or break a relationship. In fact, a lot of their dynamic could have played out because she was not happy either, and both of them felt that their needs were not being met. So, she may have intentionally withheld love from him. It's hard to say as I don't know their whole story. The main point here that I have mentioned before is that you can't get what you can't give. This is yet another big reason why relationships fail.

Emotionally crippled people tend to gravitate toward the same. This goes back to the mirror theory that I discussed earlier. Oftentimes, we can only get as much from a partner as we are able to give. Or we attract a person who will help us work through some underlying issue that needs to be addressed. This is not always a negative thing. But it can make it harder to find the beauty of love in its purest form when you are starting out wading (or swimming) in a cesspool of dysfunction. Inevitably, someone is always a better swimmer and leaves the other behind. So if you want a healthy relationship, you must first love yourself and know (and do) what fills your soul. You also have to be able to assess and take responsibility for personal challenges and be willing to work through them and make the changes to be a more authentic partner. Use baggage in the proper context: packing clothes for vacations.

> Love has nothing to do with what you are expecting to get, only with what you are expecting to give—which is everything.
>
> —(Katharine Hepburn, American actress)

Unconditional Love Meets the "If" Factor

It seems that in our quest for unconditional, divine love, we have lost focus, and love has become very conditional and extremely punitive. When our partner, child, or friend does not bend to our will, we seem to love that person less, find more judgments and faults, which slowly erodes away at the personal definition that we have assigned to our love and for our loved ones. In our unconscious thoughts, love becomes something related to cause and effect, like "I love you if [or when] you..." It is as if we are saying to people, "My love will be the reward for doing what I want you to do or being who I want you to be."

This is not love by any definition. This is ego, attachment, and control. Yet many of us continue to use these ideas interchangeably and hurt the people that we claim to love. The reality is that giving conscious or unconscious ultimatums, trying to change someone, or even hoping they will be different could not be any farther away from the truth or definition of love. We don't have to like what people do, but we have to accept them for who they are. When we don't honor people (and ourselves) for where they are on this journey we call life, the result is that most of us end up suffering in some way, shape, or form in what we have defined as love. Yet even though there seems to be so much pain attached to the notion of love, the divine did not create love for us to live in anguish. We create this sorrow with our thoughts, preconceived notions, and closed hearts. The "suffering ceases when you free your mind from attachment to things and the need to control them" (the third noble truth of Buddhism).

The pain and uncertainty of love is released when unconditional love is our guide and not the fear of a broken heart or an imperfect mate. Love grows when we realize that it surrounds us at every moment of every day. It is the sun, the trees, the barista, the cashier, and the homeless man on the street. Love is the bridge between heaven and earth. It is infinite. But so many of us feel lost, alone, angry, and end up searching for something that is as present as the air we breathe. So we become afraid that love has eluded us. With fear as the smoke screen, it is difficult to feel the love that is as close as our heart.

Fear is at the root of hate, and where there is fear and hate, you cannot have love. Love only works when we release and truly open our hearts to it. And to a greater extent, that would mean opening ourselves up to honor and respect everyone (including ourselves) on the planet for who they are, regardless of whether or not they are in alignment with our thoughts, desires, beliefs, and/or values.

Opening Up and Letting Go

When we can release the attachment to our thoughts, concepts, principles, and judgments and just be while projecting unconditional love, we can erase negativity and discord in an instant. Often times, people get disillusioned by love. They think that is is gone or unobtainable. So many people talk about all the negativity that pervades our world. Some are convinced that surely, with all the war, crime, bitterness, assault, etc., there can't be much love left on the planet. Albert Einstein said, "There is no darkness, just the absence of light." Then in the same manner, there is no hate, just an absence of love. Again, these things are not opposites; one is merely the definition of lack.

An anthropologist once asked a Hopi Indian why so many of his people's songs dealt with rain. He answered, "Because we need it so badly and it's so scarce." Then, after a moment, the Hopi said, "Why are so many of your songs about love?" (McKeever, J.) The end of the story, let go of your fears. Embrace your vulnerability. Find a way to infuse divine, unconditional love into every aspect of your life. Love is real. It is within everything and everyone on this planet. We just need to open our hearts to the possibilities. We need to let go of outdated, limiting perceptions. And, we to be vulnerable. Love has more power than anything on this planet. Without it, we perish. With it, we thrive.

> Worldly love can be like an ocean, yet an ocean has a bottom. Divine love is like the sky which is limitless. From the bottom of the ocean, soar into the vast sky.
>
> —(Sri Sri Ravi Shankar, Indian spiritual leader, advocate for nonviolence, and founder of the Art of Living)

Exactly What Is Unconditional Love?

For most of us, the idea of unconditional love transcends human understanding because the love that we have come to know and attach ourselves to is laden with ego, fear, and retributive consequences. As such, the real meaning of love becomes distorted, twisted, damaging, hurtful, and lost. The irony is that pure love is not hard to find as we are all manifestations of divine love. There is pure, divine love in everything around us—dogs, trees, nature, rocks, and other people. But because the concept has been romanticized and redefined over and over to suit our individual purposes, we can't seem to truly comprehend what is in front of us, beside us, and all around us. We don't understand that all we see *is* the manifestation of divine love. "Divine love cannot be limited by laziness. Love will make time always for others and never for your ownselves. Love suffocates on terms and conditions. Where there is an 'if' and a 'but,' true love does not exist there. Your ideal that makes you love will let you pass through all the trial of love and successfully elevate you to the level of divine love—a love that justifies no reason, a love that fears only God's approval" (Dewan, 2003). This is unconditional love.

The Face of Love is Everywhere

God is love. Love is God. We are God. As such, we are also pure love. It's just that simple. On a recent trip to India, my taxi driver reminded me of the beauty and simplicity of this concept. On his review mirror, there was a sticker that said, "Customer is God." This can be hard to grasp at the mundane level because our monkey minds want to make everything complex and overly dramatic. We also have a hard time believing in our unlimited abilities much less the potential of others. Not to mention, our egos have a one pointed focus to be right. But what we know to be true is only the truth from our own limited perspective or the experiences of others. Plus, most people tend to think and analyize too much. But that fact is also what makes life somewhat interesting.

But really, if we are honest, even if we did start to see love in everything, most of us are not inclined to call our friends to tell them of the rapturous experience we had walking through the forest, looking at the trees. Most people wouldn't even get that. They'd probably think you were high or on the verge of a nervous breakdown. Or nowadays, thanks to the advent of YouTube and instant fame, you could post a video of your experience, end up with over a million views with an offer to do a reality show. Yet love exists more powerfully in nature than in a series of dates with "the one" who gave us the feeling of butterflies in our stomach. Or if you want to experience real love in the moment, get a dog. This will give you a glimpse of the pure, divine, unfiltered love.

"Okay, So Now What?" Asks the Mind

When we open our eyes and see, really look through our hearts, we will find unconditional, pure, divine love in everything when we don't filter our senses through our intellectual mind. Once we tap into the mind, we alter what we are seeing by trying to understand and dissect it with our thoughts. All these thoughts are essentially just forms of judgment and ego. Sadly, the mind does not create a lot of pure, honest information (although I will certainly give it high marks for creativity). In actuality, our thoughts tend to run on a continuous and often frightening loop. But when we just stop and observe someone or something for what they really are (love and a manifestation of the divine), in that moment, we are connecting to that love through our hearts and attaching the object or person to our own inner divinity.

Namaste

I think this idea can be best described through the Indian word *namaste*. It literally means "I bow to you." The modern interpretation has come to be understood as "the divinity in me bows to the divinity in you." So when we genuinely use this word (or practice this concept), we are simply recognizing and honoring the interconnectedness of all beings to one another. This is love. It is seeing the world through our hearts and not with the mental chatter that comes from our brains.

Seeing and understanding life and relationships through this pure form of love is by far one of the most powerful signatures you can leave for yourself and others. Love is healing. It can help transcend mundane problems and quickly moves them to a space of compassion and understanding. Do your best to infuse love into every situation. In time, it will become a healthy habit that reaps enormous reward—more love!

> Great acts are made up of small deeds.
>
> —(Lao Tzu, father of Taoism)

What Is Love in Action?

When I lived in the United Arab Emirates, I was hired to teach human values. When I would teach the concept of love in action to schoolchildren, I would ask them, "How many of you would help somebody who had dropped their pencil case or books on the floor in the corridor?" As nearly every hand went up, I would tell them, "That is love in action." Love in action is simply service to others or service to the planet. Love in action does not have to be a grand gesture (as highlighted in my example). It is service. It is helping others. It is feeding the poor. It is an anonymous note wishing someone a great day. It is taking your extra clothes to the local mission to clothe the less fortunate.

It is taking the time to really listen to a friend in need. It can be many things, and it is God's work here on earth. Sathya Sai Baba says, "Service to others is service to God." I have also heard, "Service to others is service to self" as well as "Service to others is the rent you pay for life." However, it comes to be defined, it can be as simple as giving your smile to a stranger.

> I think dogs are the most amazing creatures; they give unconditional love. For me they are the role model for being alive.
>
> —(Gilda Radner, American comedienne and actress)

Lia

During my last year in Korea, I bought a puppy. Because of her, I have come to really understand the incredible power behind making someone smile. She is a small white Maltese. Her name is Lia (short for love in action). Typically, I am a bit of a people watcher. As such, I like to observe people as I walk around outside. As a rule, sadly, no matter where I am, I find that people rarely seem to smile and look rather rushed.

Lia is just a bundle of joy and energy. I have had strangers comment on how she is the happiest dog they've ever seen. Lia and I typically take a long walk at some point in the day. When we are out, most everyone, if even for a moment, seems to relax and smile in her presence. She brings so much happiness and laughter whenever she is out and about. She is thrilled to meet everyone. But really, she doesn't do anything special—a little lick, nibble, funny movement, or sound (that and her sheer cute factor).

Yet in those simple actions, she is providing a great service of unconditional "love in action" and living up to her name. She has no judgment and is equally open and loving to everyone. It seems that her main goal is to spread as much cheerfulness as possible as she tries her hardest to make contact with as many people and dogs as possible. Half the time, I feel like her publicist/personal assistant as I answer people's questions about the star. I often imagine how life would be if humans made the same effort to connect to others with half her enthusiasm. We would be living in a pretty fabulous world. Now truth be told, Cesar Millan would probably not approve of her overzealous and (at times) out-of-control behavior nor mine as her "pack leader" since I do little to curb her antics. But her tenacious and loving spirit is an exemplary reminder for me of how to be toward others.

Life's Examples

Many years ago, I met a man who was an environmental engineer. He wanted to make a difference in the world. I met him when I was living in Ibiza. He offered to tutor me in Spanish for free as I was not in a financial position to pay for classes. He would meet me weekly and help me in my pursuit to conquering espanol. After our class, we would talk about life. Every conversation was the same. He would go on and on about building some great big organization that helped those less fortunate in Africa. He hadn't even come close to accomplishing his lofty goals. So he felt worthless because he had not yet made a huge contribution to the world. I could see the genuine sadness in his eyes and feel his pain.

One day, we were sitting at a little café in the town center of Ibiza. We had just finished our lesson, and he had just completed another round of "I haven't helped anyone." At that point, I gently reminded him that he was helping me, the less fortunate, learn Spanish. Not only that, his job was helping to preserve the beauty and pristine landscape of the island. But what he also failed to realize was that it was a very lonely and painful time in my life. I was going through a lot of heartache over the ending of my marriage. Learning Spanish was important, but his company and friendship kept me going through my sadness. That was many years ago. Although I don't recall much of the Spanish, I still fondly remember him and am grateful for his kindness. Many people think they have to do great things to make a difference in the world. Yet it is important to remember that it can be the simplest gestures that make the greatest impact on those around us. It is important to remember that no matter the size of our efforts to genuinely serve others with love in your heart, you are doing the work of God.

Accidental Friends

While living in Madrid, I went to England for a nine-day retreat/course to immerse myself in a program that taught human values. In one of my classes, the instructor shared a beautiful story that I had heard once before. But this time, it really resonated with me. It was about a young boy who had cleaned out his locker and was walking home from school with his arms full of books. The boy was carrying so much that he ended up dropping everything on the side of the road. As he was stooping over to pick everything up, another boy from his school happened by. The boy stopped and offered to assist the young boy. The boy from school helped the young boy carry his books all the way home. They chatted a bit during the walk. And when they reached the young boy's house, the other boy asked, "Why do you have so many books?" The young boy just brushed it off that he had a lot of assignments to do. From there, the young boy invited the other boy in for a snack. They ended up talking. And over time, they became best friends.

As it turned out, the young boy was taking all his books home because he was preparing to kill himself that evening. He had been relentlessly bullied at school and had enough of the torment. The other boy's simple gesture of helping (love in action) saved the young boy's life. It wasn't until they graduated from high school that he told him the truth about his intention that fateful day in a heartwarming thank-you speech during their graduation ceremony. This story highlights a very important point about making time for others.

Without the kindness of a stranger, this story would have had a completely different ending. The sad fact is that in this rushed, fast-paced world, we barely help ourselves, much less stop to lend a helping hand for another. So the question is, "Who are you passing by?"

> Love only grows by sharing. You can only have more for yourself by giving it away to others.
> —(Brian Tracy, motivational speaker and author)

Are There Really Altruistic Acts?

Performing, serving, or offering love in action is an expression of love in its purest form (like Lia the puppy). However, there seems to be one hitch for a lot of people with regard to the whole concept of love in action. The challenge for many is to "give and do" unconditionally. This idea was famously portrayed in an old *Friends* episode where Phoebe and Joey were talking about what it meant to do a truly altruistic act. They were trying to find something that held the true essence of the definition. However, try as they might, they could not. They came to realize that the only challenge that stands in our way of this purity of love in the form of service is that we expect some type of return on our actions (unlike Lia the puppy). This happens when our ego flares up and says, "Hey, I did something for you, and now you owe me."

Granted, these thoughts are not usually a conscious thought intention. Yet typically, when we don't receive something (even a simple thank-you), our minds tend to wander off to label and judge the other person for their lack of gratitude. This is not love in action. It is merely doing out of obligation, expectation, low self-worth, or to satisfy the ego. It is not love or service prompted by inner divinity.

East vs. West

One of the things that we are trained to give ritualistically in reponse to someone's kindness are the words, "thank you." I am a strong proponent of politeness. However, I also belive that the words are used more ceremoniously than genuinely. I tend to think Americans (and other Western cultures) are a bit more stuck on the words *thank you* and *you're welcome* than in some other countries. I say this because when I was teaching English in the Korea, it was not very common to hear people use those expressions. Of course, they did from time to time. But it wasn't said for small things; it was only used for more grand gestures. As an example, when I would give my students a pen, paper, or scissors, etc., they would never say, "Thank you." At first, I thought it was because of the language barrier or they were just ill-mannered. As it turned out, doing those actions was my job. So the students did not feel obligated to thank me. For them, the same ideology would come into play if a mother prepared a meal or a father helped them with homework. It would be considered their duty. As such, no thanks are necessary.

In some ways, I think the East has a better handle on the whole issue as there are just some things we should be doing on a day-to-day basis that really don't require recognition. Some things are our duty, per se, or things we should do for others from our heart space. Doing for others should not be done as duty out of obligation but as a practice that should originate from a space of love. It is only our ego that demands that acknowledgement. Moreover, true love and service helps to move us onto our Dharmic path. If we can learn to be and do for others just for the sake of love, then love becomes its own reward. This is one of the most beautiful signatures you can leave as it helps, nurtures, loves, propagates, and teaches.

Move toward love at every turn. Use love to be your guide through life. Be love, breathe love, think about love, give love, and radiate love. Make love the focus of your existence and everything else will fall into place.

Peace

Man, today, searches for peace and contentment in false sensual pleasures entangling himself, even more, with the chains of bondage. Know, My dears, that the attachments you treasure, the pleasures you desire, the comforts you possess are nothing but the reigns of delusion that control you with the false promise of momentary happiness which will only lead you to fall, one day, from its heights into the valley of sorrows. God will never be ever touched as long as you will perceive the world as the reality and will be dependent upon its material wealth that will never sustain nor nourish the soul within. The self within suffers the pangs of hunger–Yes! The hunger of spiritual wisdom. It inflicts its deficiency on the shallow mind, making the body a diseased instrument until one is able to hear its cry of hopelessness. The deluded man turns Godward only when his mind is filled with all fears, doubts and lacks all self-confidence to face the next moment that awaits.

—Divine Messages received and recorded
by Mrs. Seema M. Dewan

Peace (Shanti)

> When we are unable to find tranquility within ourselves, it is useless to seek it elsewhere.
>
> —François de La Rochefoucauld (French novelist)

What Is Peace?

As love is the seed that sprouts all of the values, then peace can be likened to the trunk of the tree, the basis on which the other values can be nurtured and grown. In the body, peace is found in our navel region, which is considered our core. It is center proportion of da Vinci's Vitruvian man. It is the place where you build physical strength to maintain balance. Yet interestingly enough, it seems for many of us, it is what we are lacking the most. Part of the problem is that many people define peace as the absence of war or differences. When you ask them what peace looks like, people tend to hold up two fingers in a symbolic gesture.

In some regard, this is all true, but the definition is not quite correct. True peace lies within our core. It is where we come back to center when life gets out of balance. It is the value that gives us the strength and stability to support all of the other values. It is an inner calm, strength, and stillness. When we have inner peace, there isn't anything on the periphery that can bother us. We will be firm and steady throughout any storm, unwavering in the wind and rain. There is a quote by an anonymous author that beautifully describes this state: "Peace is not the absence of conflict, but the ability to cope with it."

Unfortunately, many of us are lacking peace—true inner peace. Therefore, our very foundations are shaken every time something in our lives doesn't turn out as planned. We can break a nail and feel like the world is ending when we aren't steady enough at our center to ride the waves of life. When this happens, we are thrown all over the place like a limp wet rag doll. Our emotions become roller coasters—high in one moment, but only long enough to anticipate the next drop. Then we become adrenaline junkies, waiting for our next drama fix. So to feed the drama beast, we engage in gossip, we watch reality television, or we simply create problems in our lives that don't really exist (or at least not to the degree or attention that they deserve). So for many people, they may be fine one day, and then it's all about "OMG, my world is falling apart." It is the drama that rattles us and keeps us out of our center.

> What is drama but life with the dull bits cut out.
>
> —(Alfred Hitchcock, English film director and producer)

Drama is hard to escape because we are bombarded with it on a daily basis. Think about it—going to the nail salon, hairdresser, or even for lunch with colleagues can easily be one or two hours of negativity and scandal. Stand in a checkout line, and the shelves are littered with tabloid headlines. Turn on the television, and the local news will highlight every major tragedy of the day. Every day, we are reminded in some way that we are not good enough, don't have enough, or aren't safe enough. The world around us seems to mirror our absence of peace at every turn. We can't seem to escape the restlessness that comes from our lack of inner peace. And because of this, we spread our destructive state of mind to (ironically) feel better. This is called gossip. I mean, let's face it, it's a whole lot easier to pick apart someone else's problems as opposed to addressing our own. But in the end, this only perpetuates the negative cycle of unrest that we feel deep within our core. This is also why throughout the years talk shows and reality television have become so popular. Seeing someone else's problems offers up a flicker of hope that maybe your life isn't all that bad.

The Test

Test yourself: Try sitting with someone or talking on the telephone for any length of time without complaining about something or saying anything adverse. If you are like most of the population, you will quickly find that you don't have much to say. I have tried this several times with people that I chat with over the phone. I find that it normally takes between fifteen and thirty (sixty on a good day) seconds before something negative is brought into the conversation. It can simply be the answer to "How are you?"

> If we have no peace, it is because we have forgotten that we belong to each other.
>
> —(Mother Teresa, Catholic nun and missionary)

Why Do We Do This?

Most of us are infected with an inexplicable inner turmoil that surpasses all rationality or logic. Again, it is merely because we don't have peace at our core. Our minds are lost in repetitive thoughts that are controlled by our egos, which are solely focused on attachment desires, and outcomes. Life, the people, and the things in it never seem to be enough. To try to stop the madness, we may seek professional help or indulge in all sorts of books about spirituality or that are deemed as self-help. We may even attend lectures, retreats, or seminars. These are all good in theory because many counselors and/or self-help books are well-meaning in their quest to help us attain our heart's desire. However, it is misleading to believe that we will find some lasting variation of peace and happiness in obtaining our stuff or attracting the right partner.

The people and/or books should be encouraging us to do the exact opposite. We should be learning to shut off the spout of desire and move toward inner solace. Getting more and having more isn't making us better people. It only perpetuates our desires. The world has become a place where there is a gross amount of disproportionate wealth. People are dying of hunger while others are angry because they can't get their new Ferrari in the color they want.

Some of the tools we are using to "fix ourselves" simply end up perpetuating our problems because we get stuck in our heads with our weekly shrink appointments through recitation of affirmations, mantras, and/or fixating on our outward goals and desires. Plus, the truth for some of us is that we don't want viable answers. I dare suggest that there are quite a few people on this planet who are really just looking for validation for their problems. If we are not looking for validation, we are looking for a quick way to obtain our goals without doing the work. What we fail to realize is that getting more of anything doesn't really make our problems go away. When we get more, the human tendency is to actually want more. This throws us around in the loop of desires of which we can't seem to get out. Dizzy with longing, we get sad, depressed, sullen, angry, etc., because we aren't getting whatever stuff we think we deserve. This is *not* a way to build inner peace and find comfort and happiness in what is.

It's Too Much Weight

I can relate to this all too well to getting caught in the madness of the outer reality. I have really struggled with curbing my appetite for stuff. This problem stems back to my addiction to self-help books. In an attempt to change my ways, I have tried numerous methods to stop myself from collecting more than I need. I've tried everything from "If I don't love it, I don't buy it" to "cash only" policies. Nothing seemed to work long-term. And as I have traveled a lot, I would justify my actions by saying to myself, "This is a unique item that I will never find back in the States." The final outcome was that I would usually end up having to get rid of half of what I bought because I was over my baggage allowance and could not rationalize having all my things shipped around the world until I found a permanent residence back in the States.

As such, I have wasted an enormous amount of money on things that I never used or used very little. I can't even begin to tell you about the need to outdo Imelda Marcos in the bid for the largest shoe and/or handbag collection. But the internal turmoil that I went through of *needing to have* stemmed from my lack of inner peace. I could not find peace or solace from within. As such, I used food, stuff, and other external variables to "fix" what was ailing me. As you can imagine, my quest never ended well. Although I like to look at the few trinkets I have collected during my travels, I have come to realize that most of the things that I do have left over are no longer unique or particularly special to me now. It's all just stuff at the end of the day. And now, it is stuff that needs to be dusted once a week. The things also remind me of my struggle to find peace within myself as well as keeping my spending habits in check.

My situation is not unique. Many of us are over our weight limit in the stuff department. Either we have too many pairs of shoes, ties, books, emotional baggage, extra pounds, or whatever, which is usually a result of our wavering inner peace. I am not saying there is anything wrong with having nice things. But when most of us can't figure out how to fill the void created by our lack of inner peace, we plug it up with tangible things. This is not healthy. And although both are rather decadent, neither a pair of Christian Louboutins nor an entire chocolate cake are the answer to anyone's problems.

> I deepen my experience of God through prayer, meditation, and forgiveness.
>
> —(Marianne Williamson, Spiritual teacher, author, and lecturer)

How Do We Strengthen Our Core and Find Inner Peace?

For some, meditation, Kriya breathing, yoga, and other inner "quieting" methods help balance and turn the mind off and settle us for a while. These techniques are powerful tools when used regularly. As a matter of fact, a combination of two or three would be a great way to start or end each day. Yet even if these are practiced, for most, it isn't long before the storm clouds move in, and we are back out drowning in the sea of our emotions, which can end up in raging emotional turmoil, depression, or even violence.

I am certainly not suggesting that anyone give up their practices or that they are pointless. In fact, continuous meditational practices can really help calm and center the mind, which is key to developing inner peace. Personally, I have not had a lot of success with meditation. Most of the time, my mind wanders and makes lists. I spend most of my meditation telling my thoughts to hush. But I keep at the practice because in those rare few moments of silence in between the grocery list and thinking about what I am going to have for lunch, I know that meditation is a wonderful tool for quieting my mind. As such, I forge on because I know with practice, I will get better.

Meditation is not only a proven way to successfully bring you back to center, but it also reduces stress and connects you with the divine. So what I am suggesting is that "life happens," and it can be easy to get derailed. That is why it is all that much more important to be consistent and steadfast when you find a technique that suits your personal style and needs.

If you are looking for a starting point, one suggestion to rid oneself of the seemingly never-ending internal struggles and unrest is through something called the Guided Light Meditation. It doesn't require complete silence in the mind. In fact, it allows you to be more of an active participant in the process. This particular meditation technique helps to burn away and destroy all the pervading negativity within and around us, thereby clearing up our energy fields and bringing forth inner solace (see resource page).

Sudarshan Kriya through the Art of Living Foundation is another powerful technique that supports the elimination of negativity, stress, anger, etc. Once you learn the technique, you only need fifteen to twenty-five minutes a day to complete the process.

This is a miniscule amount of time as a trade off for keeping yourself centered. The point is that you should just find something that you enjoy and that you can commit to on a regular basis. With time, you will see positive changes, even if you don't do anything else to enhance your well-being.

The Key Components

Beyond any practical outward techniques, there are two other inner practices that need to be firmly rooted in place to be wholly successful at developing inner peace. They are trusting in and surrendering to the divine. Without incorporating these two practices, long-term efforts with anything else you are doing tend to be ineffective.

> There is nothing that wastes the body like worry, and one who has any faith in God should be ashamed to worry about anything whatsoever.
>
> —(Mahatma Gandhi, nonviolent political and spiritual leader of India)

What Do "Trust and Surrender" Mean in Practical Terms?

In order to move forward without engaging turmoil in the mind or body, we have to trust. But you can't just trust without surrender. You need both to complete the process. They are symbiotic concepts. The notion is simple yet incredibly difficult to practice as you have to trust yourself, your inner divinity, the high self, the god self, God, or whatever you want to call it. You have to know, understand, and believe that right now, everything is just "exactly how it is meant to be." Know that you are being guided to do what you are supposed to do at any given moment. And then surrender those thoughts, any feelings, and the outcome to the divine by saying, "So be it." Or "It's not my will, it is God's will. Thank you for the lesson." Then know, truly know, at your core (peace) that whatever has happened was to happen, and it is for the highest good of all concerned.

Now, this certainly does not mean that we should sit in our houses and become some sort of spiritual recluses while trusting that the divine is going to bring life, love, or success to our door. It could happen. I suppose on a mundane level, the best chance you may have is for a hot single UPS person to drop off your "100 percent guaranteed to make millions at home" business kit. Since this probably isn't going to happen, trusting requires us to be an actively-aware participant in life that understand that whatever comes our way is a divine gift, even if packaged in wrapping paper of disappointment.

I was given this point very clearly one day while riding the metro in Seoul. It was rush hour, and the metro car was packed. I could not move in any direction. I felt like a cow that had been herded into a cattle car. For about fifteen minutes, I was literally wedged behind a man who was wearing a jacket made by the Hanson Company. On his hood, the logo read "There is a difference between living and being alive." I'm not sure a lot of people get that point. But that day, I did.

In fact, some people believe that to be spiritual or highly moral people, they need to give up their lives and the things that go along with it to acquire inner peace. They may also feel that to be truly spiritual, they have to be alone because they risk rejection and isolation as a result of being misunderstood. For some there is even a sense of needing to suffer to obtain divine awareness. I believe we need to be living our lives to the very fullest as we keep our values at the forefront of our minds with the strength of peace ruminating at our core. Sure, we can hide from life. For a while, it may even seem easier when we aren't having to deal with the static of life to maintain a sense of peace. But as I see it, the true test of who someone is and where they are on the spiritual barometer is being able to apply what they've learned with the greatest teacher of all—the world and everything that comes with life. It also means moving forward, trusting, and then surrendering to the fact that you are making the best decisions possible because you are using your inner guidance. It also means living a full happy life.

God provides us tons of opportunities in life. He opens innumerable doors and makes better connections than the most successful public relations firm. He is the ultimate marketing guru. But it is our responsibility to keep our eyes and hearts open so that we not only recognize the chances that God provides, but we can also act upon them. Or we can simply ignore them and spend time wondering why we are struggling.

And Then…?

We need to keep a rein on what we think, say, and do. We also need to remember that energy begets energy. We are all part of an energetic exchange. So some days we may be fueling the energetic fire or conversely dousing it with our stillness. These inconsistencies from day to day are simply the results of not being constantly centered at our core. As an example, I'm sure it goes without saying that most of us have had the experience of being around someone who inexplicably made us feel anxious and uncomfortable. Conversely, many of us have had the experience of being around someone who helped us feel calm and collected. When we lack inner peace, we get to ride the waves of emotion based on our environmental variables and the internal mind chatter. This is also when we may miss some of the openings that God presents to us. The unsteadiness and the internal prattle end up being as if several people were trying to give you directions all at once while you were driving. You can't concentrate or focus, so you end up missing your turnoff. Then you end up lost. This is what it feels like to be lacking inner peace. It is the panic of not knowing your way and feeling misplaced.

Letting inner chaos control your actions, reactions, and emotions is a signature mark that speaks volumes about us. Ask yourself, "Are you a lose cannon, a Zen monk, or a surfer riding the waves of life? Whatever your way, finding inner peace and strength not only keeps us grounded, but also from coming unhinged at the smallest upset in our realities. It helps to keep the waters calm for those around us.

Truth

What exactly is Truth? Is it the description of a 'thing seen' as one has seen it, without exaggeration or under-statement? No. or, the narration of an incident in the same word as one has heard it narrated? No. Truth elevates; it holds forth ideals; it inspires the individual and society. It is the Light that illumines one's path to God. A life inspired by Truth will enable man to live as man–not degrade oneself to the status of a lower species. There is God everywhere and there is no second entity. God is the Truth, the only Truth. God is in every article or thing, as the basis, as understanding and understandability, as the source of Divine light. Truth is the One Awareness, the One Divine Energy that activates every living being, nay, every particle of matter.

—Author Unkown

Truth (Sathya)

> You will never find yourself until you face the truth.
>
> —Pearl Bailey (American actress and singer)

What Is Truth?

Related to the body, we find the value of truth in our head. It comes from our thoughts, which manifest into words or actions. In today's world, the word *truth* has become layered in justifications and falsehoods. However, the actual definition of truth has only two meanings. There is the abstract truth and the infinite truth. The abstract is a truth that can change over time. It can be a truth that has been handed down from generation to generation based on the knowledge, doctrines, or dogmas of one or even many. It can be a feeling or fleeting thought. It can be an idea or concept. It can be something someone told you only a moment ago or many years before. Whatever it is, it is changing. As part of our evolution, ideas and beliefs change as we grow and gain more awareness in our lives.

The challenge with abstract truth is that the majority of people take it to mean something more than it is. Abstract truth is like a game of telephone. After time, and told to enough people, the stories change. Then what something started out to be becomes grossly distorted and nothing more than the interpretation of one or a collective of many people's opinions and/or judgments. This kind of truth can lead to the rise of the ego which can create power struggles, violence, and misunderstandings. It is important to remember that what we know to be the truth today will mostly likely, inevitably develop or adjust at some point in our lives. Abstact truth is only given life and validity when one or a collective agree with the same idea. But that doesn't automatically make something accurate.

I Hate Mushrooms!

As a silly example, when I was a child, I absolutely hated mushrooms and avocados. You could not get me to eat either. In graduate school, I regularly ordered pizza as part of my staple student diet. One day, my pizza was delivered with mushrooms. I was horrified and called the restaurant to have them immediately make a new pizza for me. I also asked them to please make a note on my account that said "no mushrooms ever." When the new pizza was delivered, they had a great big label stuck on the front of the box with those exact words: "No mushrooms ever." After that day, I never saw another speck of a mushroom on any of my pizzas. At the time, my truth was that I had a quite a strong aversion to mushrooms!

Interestingly enough, now that I am a little older, I have no objection to mushrooms on my pizza, and I rather enjoy avocados. In the past, as a young adult, I also thought a Porsche was the greatest car on the planet and could not wait to own one. Now, I rather fancy the Prius and the smart car as my values (and truth) have changed about the environment as well as other practical matters. In addition, there have also been people that I thought I liked or disliked through the years, only to find that my feeling (truth) changed as I learned more about them. Abstract truth is like the wind; it blows things in and out of our realities. Just as the wind blows in different directions, invariably, so does our truth. George Canning once cleverly said, "I can prove anything by statistics except the truth."

Conversely, infinite truth is an inner knowing, divinity, the inexplicable. This truth is unchanging, solid, and secure. I am not talking about dogmas or doctrines. I am talking about an inner knowing that far surpasses any information that can be given from a book or teaching. It isn't something you can really explain, and yet this truth is the highest vibration known to man. It is simplistic and complicated all in the same breath. It is a certainty that eliminates discord, disharmony, unhappiness, and any doubts that you may possess. It is a reality that quiets the mind and allows you to surrender to your inner divinity. It is the "I Am." It is God.

> Truth is by nature self-evident. As soon as you remove the cobwebs of ignorance that surround it, it shines clear.
>
> —(Mahatma Gandhi, Nonviolent political and spiritual leader of India)

Truth: The Lost Concept

In today's world, the concept of truth has become incredibly distorted. It is as if people are sincerely afraid to speak their truth and have very little understanding of what it means to be truthful or trustworthy. Think about the world we live in. We tend to lie to our family and friends in an effort not to hurt their feelings. We can't proceed in doing much of anything these days without a lawyer standing behind us to protect our truth. A person's word and handshake is no longer their bond. The gentlemen's code of honor and integrity went out of fashion right along with purple velour and leisure suits. Lies have become so prevalent that sometimes we actually forget the truth. But in fairness to the other side, many people don't want to hear the truth. They would simply prefer to feel good about what they want to think or feed the lies that they have created to blindly maneuver through their lives.

When I lived in the Emirates, I met a woman who lied about nearly everything. She lied about where she was going, what she was doing, what she thought, and how she felt. You name it, a lie was waiting on her lips. The shame was that she lied so much that the dishonesty actually became her truth. Because she had no real connection to her own truth, she was easily swayed by other people as she simply ignored and, as such, was not connected to her personal inner knowing. She was so desperate to believe the random thoughts that filtered through her mind, came from others, or (in some cases) what she saw, that she didn't have a real grasp or awareness of what she truly and innately knew at the very core of her being. In one moment, she would be adamant that the sky was blue. But if you just gave her a convincing argument for the color being green, she would change her position and start trying to convince you that she initially thought the color was green too.

The awareness she was lacking is usually defined as our high self or more commonly known as our intuition. She was also lacking positive self-regard, which we need to maintain our truth. It was sad to watch her waver in and out of abstract truths. The end result for her was an enormous amount of depression, confusion, worry, and fear. Unfortunately, this is a common reality for people as many of us tend to do this on some level or to some degree. The fact that we have the Internet, tabloid papers, scam artists, and news reports doesn't help our quest for truth. For some, whatever they read or hear becomes an automatic truth. Then we validate ourselves by saying things like, "I read it on the Internet."

When we rely heavily on other people's truths, we deny our divinity, inner knowing, the "little voice," and then do, say, or even sometimes feel what is not for our highest good or well-being. Once we are in denial of our truth, we become lost in the illusion of what really is with regard to ourselves and others. Consequently, we may try to project our truth on to others in an attempt to find comfort for ourselves, deny, or even try to avoid what is really going on in our lives or in our minds.

The Mass Exodus

This rejection of our intuition and divinity has led to a mass exodus from the truth. As a result, there are people all over the planet fighting for things where they have no real understanding of what they are actually fighting for. In many cases, it is simply a political, generational, or cultural battle that has ensued over time without any real moral grounds. As a result, we have people convicting, persecuting, harming, or killing others based on antiquated facts and outdated concepts. We forget that it wasn't all that long ago where people once thought the world was flat, the earth was the center of the universe, and we shouldn't eat eggs. These were all abstract truths.

> Your time is limited, so don't waste it living someone else's life. Don't be trapped by dogma—which is living with the results of other people's thinking. Don't let the noise of other's opinions drown out your own inner voice. And most important, have the courage to follow your heart and intuition. They somehow already know what you truly want to become. Everything else is secondary.
>
> —(Steve Jobs, American entrepreneur, marketer, and inventor)

The Sheep Mentality

During my last year in Korea, I seriously considered staying in the country long-term. I love the country, have great friends there, and wasn't sure about how I would fit back into American culture after being gone for so long. So I decided that it was time to introduce the values. I was excited to share these concepts with the masses. But I needed to create a business platform. However, after my disaster of 2002, I knew I needed the right tools to get solid and safe footing to do that. To prepare myself, I took a two-week global business course to understand what I would need to do to be successful in my endeavors. One day after our class, the speaker (a Westerner) asked me what I wanted to do. I told him, "I want to teach human values—love, truth, peace, right conduct, and nonviolence." He promptly responded, "Good luck with that. There is no concept of truth in this culture. It is considered [and encouraged] acceptable to lie if it saves face or keeps the honor of the family name."

This experience highlighted what I define as the sheep mentality. There are generations of people who have no or very little idea about how to tap into themselves or their inner guidance. They just do and say things because that is the way it has been done. So what has ended up happening is that we have generation after generation of people pleasers working to make everyone but themselves happy. What's worse is that we have learned to strategically lie to ourselves as justification for our actions. We say things to ourselves like "I couldn't tell her the truth because I didn't want to hurt her feelings"; "I didn't need to go to the gym today. I walked a lot at work"; Yes, I know I told myself I wasn't going to have any more doughnuts, but today has been a particularly difficult day for me. I deserve a treat! My diet can start tomorrow"; "I know I told myself I'd complete that project, but I haven't sat down all day today. I need a break"; "She hurt my feelings, but it's okay." "I don't know why people keep saying I am rude. Jim is far more inconsiderate than I could ever be"; or "I had every right to attack him; he was nasty to me first." For many of us, the biggest lie that we tell ourselves is "I'm happy."

We spend most of our days deceiving ourselves because we have unconsciously come to understand that if and when we face the truth, we must face ourselves. Since this is never very comfortable or easy, blame, denial, and deception become the escape from looking at ourselves in the magnified mirror. Living in our truth takes great strength of character and responsibility for our actions. It means living with conscious awareness. It can also mean making great changes or even sacrifices. It also means being potentially uncomfortable. Because telling the truth can be such a scary notion, lying to ourselves becomes a mainstay in most people's lives. Why shake the apple and run the risk of being hit with falling apples? But the fact of the matter is if we can't be honest with ourselves, how can we possibly be honest with others?

In a December 2012 issue, *Women's Health* magazine addressed a study done by the University of Notre Dame. The study pointed out that people lie an average of eleven times per week. The researcher asked the study participants to refrain from lying for ten weeks. The results: people who were honest reported fewer sore throats and mental tension. Researcher Anita Kelly, PhD, said, "When they told few lies, their relationships improved, which is why their health improved too." Telling the truth is not just about good moral character; it is about building authentic relationships too.

> Children and drunks always speak the truth.
>
> —(Proverb)

Telling a lie has more to do with what is going on inside you than the situation at hand.

I enjoy listening to very young children. Before they are touched by the disease of dishonesty, when a young child tells you, "You are beautiful," it is coming from a place of innocence and beauty. Children also have no qualms about asking someone something very direct and against what would be considered politically or socially correct. The thing with children is that their words aren't being filtered through the intellect. They aren't wondering, "How will this person feel when I say this?" What they say is as they know it to be or how they feel in that moment.

They stare when they don't understand what they see. They ask questions when they don't know the answers. They cry when they are hurt. They take food when they are hungry. There is no social formality that "rejects an offer or keeps their feelings in" because it will make them seem stronger and polite instead of weak and troublesome. Think about how many times you have rejected someone's offer not because you didn't want their help or what they had for you, but because what your truth was really saying is "I don't deserve the help" or "I need help, but I don't want people to think that I am weak," or "I would love that piece of chocolate, but I don't want people to think that I am easily tempted or actually even eat chocolate."

> A lie can travel half way around the world while the truth is just putting on its shoes.
>
> —(Mark Twain, American writer and humorist)

Where Did We Get Lost from Truth?

A very dear Spanish friend of mine gave me his perspective of what truth meant. He said, "In Spain, we say 'a lie has short legs.' This means you can't get very far with a lie because someday the truth will prevail. If someone builds the foundation of their house on a lie, as they become older, they risk being discovered. Truth always comes up higher than the foundation, and the effects are more devastating."

But then he went on to say, "However, some lies are needed. We cannot say that our behavior in response to a situation must be by the book. What we say can depend upon who we have in front of us as well as the situation. Sometimes, one has to evaluate the circumstances before they decide what to say. We also have to assess if the truth will have more severe consequences than the lie. Sometimes a white lie disguises a terrible truth. So it is not always necessary to tell the truth."

My response to him was, "Huh?" His logic had completely contradicted itself.

This Is Where We Got Lost

This is where we got lost in the value of truth. We got lost when we started to convince ourselves of phrases like "It's just a little white lie" and when we decided that truth only mattered if it didn't hurt anybody or helped us navigate a situation. And as a society, we have bought into and perpetuated the idea of lies and untruths through our purchase of gossip magazines and use of social networking. Through these new media forms, people can create a façade, embellish the truth, or "catfish" someone completely. Yet through all the justification of why we lie or believing "it must be true because I read it or someone said it," we forgot one very important variable: without truth, we only hurt ourselves and invariably those around us.

Without truth, we can't truly grow and change. Without truth, our lives are empty and meaningless distortions of what really is. Then we end up living in a world based on the fear of others, finding out who we really are and how we really feel. We live in a world where we lie to the people who we proclaim to love. We live in a world where we have to ferret through gossip and half-truths to find a glimmer of fact. We live in a world where we lie to and deceive ourselves. As one anonymous author said, "Unless your heart, your soul, and your whole being are behind every decision you make, the words from your mouth will be empty, and each action will be meaningless. Truth and confidence are the roots of happiness."

> The biggest consequence to telling a lie is, it leads you to telling another one.
>
> —(Gary King, Attorney General of New Mexico)

Why Is It Difficult to Live Our Truth?

In my human values classes, I would ask the children, "Why are we afraid sometimes to tell the truth?" Their answers were always the same. "I don't want to get in trouble. I am afraid I am going to get punished." Interestingly enough, these excuses are not exclusive to children. These are also some of the exact same reasons why adults lie. But we can add a few more to the list: "I am afraid they will love/like me less. I am afraid that they will leave me. I am afraid they will find out who I really am. I am afraid they will judge me. I am afraid he/she will never call me again." And on and on.

When asked what were the biggest reasons why adults lie, University of Massachusetts psychologist Robert Feldman said, "It's tied in with self-esteem. We find that as soon as people feel that their self-esteem is threatened, they immediately begin to lie at higher levels." If we check in and really see lying for what it is, we will come to understand that it is a silly way to behave and respond. It denies your worth as well as who you really are. And it certainly does not allow for you to live with integrity. So when we lie, the hard reality is that it is because we simply have little or low self-respect or self-regard for ourselves as well as for those around us. If we truly honored ourselves and each other's inner divinity, lying would seem wholly unnatural.

How Do We Get Back to the Truth?

A dear friend of mine has said to me a number of times, "You can say anything to anyone. It is just how you say it." I still have not figured out exactly how to do that as I believe true diplomacy is a fine art where words become like paint to a canvas. In the end, the "picture" can be refined poetry or an auditory disaster. I also find that a big part of what you say and how it is received has a lot to do with the mood, state of being, etc., of yourself and your audience. Regardless of all of this, it is critical to have impeccability with our words and our thoughts. What we think, whether it is the truth or a lie, if it is rattling around in our head, it is just waiting for a stage cue to exit our mouths. This is why it is important to always be in alignment with your thoughts, words, and actions. All of these must be in harmony for one to be in their truth at all times. Without just one of these components not in order with all the rest, you are simply not being sincere. Remember that having a signature that says you are trustworthy and honest is essential to forming authentic, lasting relationships with yourself and those around you.

Let go of the illusion of control.
—(Master Oogway, Kung Fu Panda)

Panda Wisdom

It seems that the more we try to grasp for God (infinite truth), the farther He gets from our reach. We must let go and release all ideas, concepts, or notions that we hold on to about what *truth* is. It is only when we are free from our limited constructs (including the truth we hold about reaching God) that we can fully go back to our original nature—back to the basics.

A perfect example of this was shown in the movie *Kung Fu Panda*. Po was a simple panda. Because of his childlike, simplistic nature, it was easy for him to find his true potential because he possessed innocence and purity. He wasn't bogged down with trainings, teachings, seminars, or random notions. As such, he was more free to find his way to becoming the Dragon Warrior (God potential). But he also had to let go of any limiting ideas related to what he thought it meant to be the Dragon Warrior. As Po came to find out in the end, "there is no secret ingredient." Po had to release the limited constructs of the external to find his own inner strength (inner divinity). In essence, the message was there isn't anything but what we have within us (the core human values) that can lead us to who we truly are—infinite truth (God).

Oprah Winfrey once said, "Truth allows you to live with integrity. Everything you do and say shows the world who you really are. Let it be the Truth." It is important not limit your potential with outdated and antiquated ideas of who and what you are. Sathya Sai Baba once said, "You can't oblige everyone, but you can speak obligingly." Open yourself up to the possibilities. Live free from the fear of deceit and falsehood. Speak, live, and be truth.

Right Conduct

When I was young and had all energies, I wanted to change the world. I found it difficult to change the world, so I tried to change my nation. When I realized that the nation was too large a place, I began to focus on my town. I couldn't even change the town and so I decided that changing my family would be sufficient. Now, on my deathbed, I know that the only thing I can change is myself.

Suddenly I realize that if, long ago, I had changed myself, I could have impacted my family. With its support, I could have made an impact on our town. That impact could have changed the nation and, who knows, one day I could indeed have changed the world!

—The epitaph of a 12th century monk

Right Conduct (Dharma)

It's not hard to make decisions when you know what your values are.

—Roy Disney (The Walt Disney Company)

What Is Right Conduct?

Right conduct is something similar to the scales of justice—one side being good choices, the other side bad decisions. If you are a cartoon fan, this has been depicted as the angel and the devil that sit on the shoulders of the main character, trying to convince them of what to do. Except in the case of right conduct, the angel always wins.

The central idea behind right conduct is purely about making good choices. However, there are several factors that need to be considered when making good decisions. Primarily, they consist of thinking about how a choice will impact one's own well-being as well as those around you. Doing the right thing is not right conduct if you are not taking others or the planet into consideration during your decision-making process. For example, taking a new job may bring you more money, but you may end up spending less time with your loved ones. It is important to weigh out the options and take an honest look at the long-term and short-term consequences of your actions. From there, responding in a way that is for the benefit of everyone is the essence of this value.

However, right conduct is about more than making mundane choices. It is also about taking care of yourself and not wasting time, energy, food, or money. These are all precious resources that need to be used wisely and with great consideration. In addition, right conduct is about teaching and giving respect to others. It is also educating children about the value of their parents and teachers.

Old-School Philosophies

I remember as a child, my parents were adamant about me calling anyone older than me Mr. or Mrs. I was never allowed to call an elder by their first name (even if they asked me to). This habit followed me into adulthood. I still have a hard time just calling people older than me by their first names. Although is it becoming easier as my own numerical value (age) increases.

As I have mentioned, for some time, I lived in South Korea. It is a culture steeped in the ideas of respect and tradition. There is a hierarchy that is followed in the way Koreans speak and interact. These philosophies are even imbedded into the structure of their spoken language. When I lived there, I found this to be refreshing (apart from being asked my age all the time to establish my level of seniority). I have also had the good fortune to live in other countries around the world and witness the vast differences between people (more specifically the children) from Eastern countries from those of Western countries.

For the most part, what I witnessed was that there are principles and discipline in the East and chaos and confusion in the West. On the whole, children from the Eastern and the Western parts of the world primarily do the same things: play violent video games, listen to rock music, eat junk food, etc. But the difference is that for many from the East, the values of respect and honor are reinforced in their culture, homes, and schools of the children. Sadly, however, things have been changing over the past few years due to an increase in Western influence. But for the most part, not all that long ago, a Korean child would not even consider talking back to an adult or using informal language with an elder. Conversely, children in the West tend to talk to adults like they talk to their friends (and sometimes without even that level of respect). This is not right conduct!

We should be teaching children early on through words, actions, and examples the benefits and necessity of honoring and respecting each other, especially their parents and teachers. As parents, teachers, and members of society, it is our duty to model these healthy behaviors. If children can't respect their parents (or caregivers), how will they be able to value themselves or other people who come into their lives?

> Manners easily and rapidly mature into morals.
> —(Horace Mann, American education reformer)

It Is about Something More Than Just Making Good Choices

Right conduct is about more than just making good choices. It is also a basic code of conduct for being polite and respectful to those (and nature) around you. Although there seems to be somewhat of an alternate message being delivered in today's society, there is no glamour in pushing, shoving, or cheating our way through life. But this kind of behavior is shown around the clock on our television shows. Society is actually encouraging and paying to see people belittle, bully, abuse, etc., each other as well as themselves on TV. It is mind-boggling, and yet we wonder why some children are so ill-mannered and morally bankrupt.

> There's no chivalry in culture any more. Sometimes you meet someone who everyone says is polite and you're like, "Wow," but then it's like, "Hang on, isn't everyone supposed to be polite?"
>
> —(Will.i.am, American recording artist and songwriter)

Showing good manners and having genuine, proper etiquette is not only polite, it is necessary to maintain good relations with others. It is a way to coexist peacefully with those around us. It also shows a level of elegance, sophistication, and respect when we give up our seat on the bus for someone elderly, pregnant, etc., hold a door open, or genuinely use *please*, *thank you*, *you're welcome*, and other polite phrases and actions. Maybe in some ways I am old-fashioned, but I find it endearing and chivalrous when a man opens my car door or waits for me to walk through the door first. The point is, good manners can take you a long way! But more than the social impact of being polite and making good choices, there is a physiological implication too. It can create a sense of tranquility.

Anaid Heyd, an eHow contributor, said in an article, "Good decisions foster a tranquil state of mind, one that is less stressed or worried about the future. Individuals who make bad decisions worry about the repercussions of their actions, especially if they led to illegal activities. They may fear law enforcement agencies or public judgment, thereby inhibiting their ability to enjoy their personal lives. Those who make the right decisions, on the other hand, can relax, knowing that they have not done anything wrong. Future prospects are much brighter for those who have chosen well, including better career options and overall life satisfaction."

> Time is the coin of your life. It is the only coin you have, and only you can determine how it will be spent. Be careful lest you let other people spend it for you.
>
> —(Carl Sandburg, American writer and editor)

Using Time Wisely

Time and our life are the greatest gifts we have been given by the divine. Many of us waste time exponentially. Yet ironically, most people say that they don't have enough time. The September–October 2005 issue of *The Futurist* examines Americans' use of time. According to the article, "The common perception that there just isn't enough time isn't supported by the stats from a national study using time-diaries. Basically, the findings show that Americans average 35 hours per week of work time and 35 hours per week of free time. This is much more time than what most Americans perceive." The article goes on to say that half of an adult's leisure time is spent in front of the television. So ultimately, how one spends their time determines how they feel about the quality of their free time and, paradoxically, their lives.

> To affect the quality of the day, that is the highest of arts.
>
> —(Henry David Thoreau, American author, poet, and philosopher)

Quality vs. Quantity

I read a statistic that stated the average American father spends approximately twelve minutes a day of quality time with his children. Another source on the web said 2.5 hours a day. But they did not quantify that time as quality. In that time span, they listed activities like shopping, watching television, etc. I have also read that the average American spends up to four and a half hours a day in front of the television. That is just over thirty-two hours a week in front of a TV. In some cases, that is more time than what children spend with their teachers in school. But if it is not more time, it is certainly about the same amount of time that they spend in a learning environment. Either way, in my assessment, it is too much television.

These statistics also highlight the fact that we are not using our time to create quality moments for ourselves or our loved one. Moreover, we are wasting time exponentially on things that have very little value or meaning for our overall existence. A more poignant point to consider is that research has shown that watching too much television decreases intelligence levels, reduce one's ability to concentrate, and in extreme cases, one can develop neurodegenrative brain disorders.

Shortly after I moved in the Park in Missouri, my friend's television got fried in a lightning storm. Neither of us was in a financial position to buy another one. All I kept thinking was, "What am I going to do with myself?" It ended up that we didn't have a television for a year. As I mentioned early in the book, in that year, I have never been so productive or creative. I learned how to crochet. I made furniture and jewelry. I read some incredibly inspiring books, studied quantum physics, helped remodel a house, exercised, and finished my doctoral dissertation in spiritual counseling. I had to quickly learn that there is quality life beyond television.

Technology, the Master Time Waster

With the advent of technology, the Internet, Facebook, video games, and other distractions, we have become master time wasters. It has been suggested that what you do in your free time defines who you truly are as a person. For some, this could be an arguable claim. But yet if we are honest, for many of us, there are so many more productive ways that we can spend our free time. For most, it is easy to justify, "I work hard all week. I just need to relax." Sure, that may be true. But if we look at what we are working for and are honest with ourselves, generally, we are employed to obtain stuff or to pay for our stuff. For most of us, we are not working purely to meet our basic needs. We are working to get a better mobile phone, larger television, newer car, bigger home, take a family trip, etc.

As I see it, we would not need more cell phone minutes or larger text plans if we simply learned how to spend quality time in direct contact with our friends and families. Moreover, many families and people tend to use the once-a-year vacation to escape their lives. We would not be so excited to take an annual family holiday if we learned to enjoy and embrace each and every day. But we have lost the simple art of personal bonding and camaraderie. So it's no wonder we need to pay for ways to communicate and connect with ourselves and loved ones. But is it all really necessary? And in the end, wouldn't our time be better spent in service to others or having meaningful interactions, not playing Candy Crush on Facebook?

The Siesta

I lived in Spain for several years. In that time, I learned to appreciate the fine art of mealtime. As many people know, the Spanish have a siesta over lunch. In some circumstances, people do actually rest. But in most cases, this is a time to have a long relaxing lunch with colleagues or friends.

I recall my first few lunch outings in Spain. I was trying to rush the waiter so that I could get back to work or do something else. My efforts were futile as there is a natural timing that comes with Spanish lunch service, and either you adhere to the rules or you end up frustrated. Those are really the only two choices because nothing is going to happen any faster. What I came to learn over time is to slow down and enjoy the experience of the food and my company. But the sad fact was that most of us don't even sit down to a family meal. In fact, many of us eat on the go. I think we all need to incorporate a daily family and friend's siesta time into our lives. If done with love and commitment, it could quickly recharge the energy and dynamic of the family infrastructure.

What about Wasting Food?

Let's face it, most of us eat far too much and waste even more. Stop and think about how much you throw away on a daily or weekly basis. This is not a problem exclusive to countries like the United States or England. This is a problem of epic proportions in all industrialized countries. For many of us, food is a very big and consuming part of each day. And because we have easy access to everything, we end up buying too much, and we rarely take into consideration how much we actually need. We buy things with good intentions or because it is on sale and at weeks' end, a portion of it ends up in the garbage. This is especially prevalent with fruits and vegetables.

I read on a website called Love Food Hate Waste that homes in the United Kingdom throw away 8 million tons of food every year. In the States, the numbers differ. But it is suggested that between 14 and 17 percent of all the food purchased is wasted. Not only is throwing food away a waste of our money and resources, it is responsible for an enormous amount of the carbon dioxide emissions from landfills.

Beyond the carbon footprint, eating too much food is damaging to our health and well-being. This is evident in the amount of diseases that are plaguing developed nations. To highlight this, according to the National Diabetes Information Clearinghouse (NDIC), "Diabetes affects 8.3 percent of the United States population. The Center for Disease Control (CDC) recorded that 12 percent of all non-institutionalized adults are diagnosed with heart disease." That is over 20 percent of the United States population. If we look at the culprit in many (or most) cases, it is too much food. A lot of that comes in the form of refined sugars, white flour, and chemically preserved, genetically modified food!

Food Addiction

I personally know all too well about the dependence on and misuse of food. Food was my nemesis for most of my life. The dysfunctional relationship began when I was a child where food was used for reward as well as punishment. If I was bad, I was sent to my room without dinner. If I was good, I was allowed some kind of treat. Food was the proverbial carrot that was dangling in front of me based on my performance. Since then, as an adult, I used food to stuff feelings, fill emptiness, reward behaviors, etc. Food became an obsession. I lived to eat, forgetting that I only needed to eat to live. My weight yo-yoed. I am fortunate that I am tall, so the impact has tended to be aesthetically minimal. The biggest effect of my challenge was that my mind was unsettled. I was always unhappy with my weight. I felt guilt for overeating, which led to excessive dieting and working out. I even tried bulimia. Fortunately, what I found is that my inability to commit to things became a blessing in that instance. As a result of the poor choices I made and the ways that I chose to deal with food and, to a greater extent, my emotions, this led to a series of physical ailments. So after years of doing battle with food, I finally realized that I was terribly unhappy with the power that it held over me. I needed a plan. I had to stop feeding Milan and start feeding God.

At the time, I could not make the complete connection to my inner divinity, nor did I understand what need the food was meeting for me. So I used the separate form of God in my strategy to get control over my addiction. From there, whenever I thought about eating something unhealthy or stuffing myself, I simply asked myself two questions: "What are you feeling right now? And would you feed or do this to God?" Since most of my food choices were not worthy of God's plate, it was easy to put things down out of love for the divine until I found that same love feeling for myself. In addition, as a general rule, consuming food when you're emotional is the worst time to eat as from a quantum perspective, your thoughts change the vibration of your food. So if you are feeling sad, your food will become sadness. If you feel guilt for eating something, you are more likely to gain weight as guilt is an emotion that you keep in, not release. Linked that

that idea, you should not eat food while watching or listening to anything violent or while under stress. This will also change the vibration of your food as well as your state of being.

The idea of food and water having a vibration was brought to the forefront by Dr. Masaru Emoto. He claimed that human emotions can alter a water molecule. To prove this, he used words, music, prayer, etc., with water to see what would happen to the water molecule. After exposing the water to the different vibrations, he froze it and took pictures with a high-powered microscope. What he found was that the water molecules exposed to positive words, beautiful music, etc., came out as awe-inspiring crystals. The water that was exposed to negativity photographed as diseased, distorted crystals. His work highlights the fact that we have an enormous impact over the state of our bodies (as we are between 60–70 percent water). But he also showed the public that our thoughts can influence what we take in to nourish our bodies too. So it is important to be impeccable with our words. But more than that, do not prepare food or ingest it while you are in a negative state. It goes back to a very old saying, "You are what you eat." Be mindful of what you put into your body.

Take the Pressure Off Yourself

Dealing with food and emotions in a healthy way starts with taking the pressure off ourselves to be thin and perfect and redirecting the focus on being healthy. For myself and the vast majority of others who struggle with food issues, the real question is, What was eating at me as the real problem is not about what I am eating? We need to really figure out our trigger points without actually pulling the trigger. Once we are more consciously aware of our feelings and emotions, we have to learn to feel the sensation and then, like a cloud in the sky, observe it and let it pass. If we take more time to live in conscious awareness and not just mindlessly wander through our day or to the refrigerator, we will be wholly more successful at taking care of the vehicle we define as our body.

> Teaching a child not to step on a caterpillar is as valuable to the child as it is to the caterpillar.
> —(John Robbins, author of Diet for a New America)

Living with a Conscience

Living in the value of right conduct is about moderation, balance, healthy choices, and doing what is the best for everyone (not just a temporary fix to quickly or easily resolve a feeling or a problem). It is important to remember that when we take food from the market that we are not going to eat, we (in essence) take that food from someone else. When we (in general) eat or overconsume meat, we contribute to hunger in Third World countries and the devastation of the rain forests. We must consider our choices so that we are not contributing to unnecessary waste and/or planetary destruction.

How Does That Happen?

Things on the planet have become very imbalanced. There are ways to move back to a more positive balanced center. In point of fact, we can make minor changes that would drastically reduce world hunger and global ruin. According to an article written in the late 90s called "Meat and the Environment," "The world's cattle alone consume a quantity of food equal to the caloric needs of 8.7 billion people—more than the entire human population on Earth." Furthermore, the environmental think tank, Worldwatch Institute stated, "The easiest way to reduce grain consumption is to lower the intake of meat and milk, grain-intensive foods. Roughly 2 of every 5 tons of grain produced in the world are fed to livestock, poultry, or fish; decreasing consumption of these products, especially of beef, could free up massive quantities of grain and reduce pressure on land."

In addition, when we purchase things that are prepackaged or in plastic, we are contributing to the degradation of the planet and cruelty to animals. More than the global and environmental factors, when we overeat or eat poorly, we damage our bodies and our minds. Right conduct is the value that has the most noticeable, telltale impact on ourselves and everything around us.

What Is Meant by Wasting Energy and Resources?

Of course, we can waste energy and resources in the literal form by not shutting off lights, taking long showers, or not shutting off water when we aren't using it. We can also stop driving two blocks to the market when we can just as easily walk there. But there is a deeper meaning with regard to waste. It means expending our energy on things that don't have any value. For example, we waste our energy (and time) by surfing the Internet for endless hours or watching too much television. Or we talk more than we need to and often say absolutely meaningless things that contribute to negativity and gossip.

The spiritual leader Sathya Sai Baba once said, "The silent man has no enemies." You can't argue with that simple logic because I think most of us would agree that to some degree or another, it is our words that get us in the most trouble. More than that, using empty words or just filling the silence with meaningless chatter is a waste of our energy. Oftentimes, the need to talk for no reason or fill the silence comes from a lack of inner peace. Some think that just because they are in the car with someone, they need to have a conversation or something is wrong. Of course, at times, this may be the case, but when the values are in alignment, silence is golden.

Checklist

If you are struggling with how you use your words, have communication issues, or just want to practice discernment, there is a way to monitor the necessity of what you are about to say. It has been suggested that before you speak, ask yourself the following questions: Is what I am about to say kind? Is it necessary to say it? Is it true, or just a momentary abstract truth? If you can answer yes to all of those questions, then finally ask yourself, Is what I am about to say going to improve upon the silence? Using these questions to gauge your words is an excellent way to avoid meaningless chitchat that often does more harm than good.

The Anti-Checklist

During my time in Korea, I met a woman who was in a dead-end relationship. She had been with her boyfriend for six years, and he was giving her all the signals that it was over. She knew it was coming to an end. She also knew that it was just a matter of time before they would finally separate. However, she would not let go of him. To make matters worse, he was married and had never had any intention of getting divorced from his wife. As such, she wasted countless hours, days, months, and years ruminating over the fate of their nonexistent relationship as well as going through an enormous amount of emotional turmoil. Moreover, he did all of this for a man who already had a spouse. She incessantly talked to anyone who would listen about "their troubles," always coming back to the same resolve: "it was over." Even though all the signs were clear and the relationship was by all accounts unhealthy, she continued to engage in countless futile arguments with the man even though he was making his dissatisfaction about the relationship rather apparent to her.

Her friends sat with her for endless hours rehashing her feelings and giving her advice. People tried to be supportive, give her compliments and reassurance. Yet she was not willing to give up the dysfunction that was defining her life. The drama was meeting her human needs at a very deep level. As such, she wasn't ready to give up her story as that would have only exacerbated her feelings of insignificance. She could not see her own value and was making poor choices to satiate her desires.

This is and was a colossal waste of time and energy for her, the man, and all the people she burdened with her tales of drama. Not only that, the overall dynamics and back story of the situation broke all of the other values of love, truth, peace, and nonviolence. Moreover, sharing her tales of infidelity with the world are certainly not doing anything to enhance her reputation or, as we have called it, her signature. Holding on to things or relationships that are no longer in harmony or are our best interest is not only a waste but also a disservice to you and anyone involved. Moreover, talking about things that only make people uncomfortable or leave them feeling distressed is also not right conduct.

You Can't Always Replicate

Our time and energy as well as the precious resources that we need to fuel our lives must be cherished as they are finite in nature. This includes all the things that positively affect our health and mental well-being (as well as that of others). There is nothing man-made that can truly replicate what God has given us. As such, we should use everything in moderation and with consideration for the planet and everyone around us. If we don't take these things into consideration now, we won't even have them to consider in the future. What choices do you make? And what do they say about you?

> For each new morning with its light,
> For rest and shelter of the night,
> For health and food, for love and friends,
> For everything Thy goodness sends.
> —(Ralph Waldo Emerson, American essayist)

The Attitude of Gratitude

Without question, one of the only real ways forward for us and our planet is to put a limitation on our desires. Most of us work countless hours to buy and pay for our stuff. Many of us spend time away from our families to give them what is defined as "a better life." As a result, there probably aren't too many people who don't have something in their house that they bought and never used. We are a society of mass consumerism. Nothing is ever enough. We need the latest, the biggest, the greatest, the only, the fanciest, the youngest. This begs the question, When is enough, enough?

It all becomes sufficient or enough when we take the time to really be thankful for the things that we have: the people in our lives, our bodies as they are, and our existence in general. When we can come to a place of peace and of gratitude for everything (good, bad, or indifferent) that comes into our world, then the idea of lack becomes less predominant and eventually nonexistent. But in the wanting, we tend to forget what is right in front of us. Look around you. Are you okay? If you are breathing and alive, you are okay in this moment. So essentially, everything else is a gift of abundance no matter how small it may, in fact, seem to you right now.

The truth is that there aren't many of us who have the right to complain. Our egos want to complain. They are hardwired to complain. Some are even stuck on an automatic loop of grievances. But that isn't the truth of most of our lives. Most of us have more than enough. In fact, the United States and the United Kingdom are two of the five wealthiest countries in the world. A significant portion of the 6.8 billion people on our planet live on less the $3.00 per day. More often than not, people don't have proper shelter, food, water, or lack adequate eduction (in any at all). As a country, we are rather blessed by all that we have so readily available to us at any given moment. So in reality, if you check in with yourself and take the time to think about what you have, you will find, in this moment, it is probably more than enough.

There is a funny quote that highlights our loss of gratitude for the simple things. It was G. K. Chesterton who said, "When we were children, we were grateful to those who filled our stockings at Christmastime. Why are we not grateful to God for filling our stockings with legs?"

> Be content with what you have; rejoice in the way things are. When you realize there is nothing lacking, the whole world belongs to you.
>
> —(Lao Tzu, father of Taoism)

Persona Non Grata (the Ego Self)

I personally have to keep myself in check about my attitude of gratitude. I have had my share of ups and downs. I have been at the lowest point where I had almost nothing left but my health. I had nobody and nothing to speak of and was scrimping to eat and take care of the daily essentials. Yet even in that darkest night of my soul, I was physically healthy and had a roof over my head. Fast-forward many years later, I was, according to my ego, having a particularly rough patch in my life. I wasn't anywhere near where I had been in my darkest times, but I felt sorry for myself and was angry and depressed. My ego had a hold over me. I had lost the joy and happiness that comes from living in love and connection with all that was around me.

While I was living in Seoul, I essentially had it made. I had a good job, free apartment, relaxed schedule, and overall easy life. It was Saturday, my me day. But for some reason, the free apartment, disposable income, and stress-free life just weren't enough. That afternoon, I was coming out of a spa where I just had some wonderful treatments done. I got home and, for some elusive reason, was angrily putting away the purchases of the day. Sadness had become such a standard response in my life that I could easily go there without any particularly valid reason. All of a sudden, I had a moment of clarity. In that instant, I stopped what I was doing and said to myself (my ego), "Excuse me! Ego, you just had a fabulous massage. You want for nothing. You have a place to live and food to eat. In essence, your life is great! What exactly are you complaining about?"

In that moment, I took account of everything that was in my life. Nothing in my life was bad, wrong, or so difficult. It was all right. It was my thinking that was incorrect. Everything in my life was good, wonderful really, and exactly how it was supposed to be in that moment. With God's love to guide me and Him always by my side, how could my world go wrong? All of a sudden, all of my seemingly insurmountable problems had a massive spotlight shining down on them. And I could clearly see that the many challenges that I had gotten lost in and gave my strength, power, thought, and time to were rather petty and quite insignificant in the scheme of things. With that new understanding and feeling of gratitude, there came lightness, freedom, and an inner silence.

Learning to take into account and be grateful for what and who are in your life is life-changing because it gives less credence to what you don't have. But more than that, when we get caught in the trap of the ego, we separate from our divinity. We are everything, and everything is us. So nothing is bad when you view it with love. Let gratitude be your driving force, not fear or desire. This is the personification of right conduct.

Nonviolence

"Anger"-the poisonous venom that spreads its death from the mind to the senses and from the senses to your actions. Know that the seed of anger can be curbed from its growth, right from the beginning stages, by recognizing its evil, rejecting it, and draining its flow in the gutters that will flow away from the pure nectar of stability and patience. Behind each act of anger, lies the secret of desire that cries in its fear of remaining unfulfilled.

—Living in the Presence of God, Volume 1

Nonviolence (Ahimsa)

> Violence is not merely killing another. It is violence when we use a sharp word, when we make a gesture to brush another away, when we obey because there is fear.
>
> —Jiddu Krishnamurti (writer and speaker on philosophical and spiritual issues)

A Case of Mistaken Identity

Typically, violence is primarily identified with crime, war, and killing. Yet some of the biggest acts of violence are committed with words, not actions. Beyond that, the greatest violations usually occur against ourselves. This comes in the form of verbal abuse more commonly known as negative self-talk. It sounds something like "I am so stupid," "I'm such an idiot," "Why can't I do anything right?" "I am so fat," "Nobody loves me," "What's wrong with me?"

Abusing ourselves with words is violence in the worst form as it is something that we do *not* have to endure. It is completely an act committed by us, toward us. Although this kind of violence is completely avoidable, most of us mistreat ourselves each and every day (and usually unknowingly).

The second kind of violence occurs when we turn our unkind words toward others. This happens every day in some form or another. This occurs when we belittle, judge, blame, or misdirect our emotions toward another.

As a rule, we learn that words only have the power that we or others give them. So theoretically, people can't be hurt by what someone says to them unless they allow the words to create pain and discomfort. So the challenge with the whole "sticks and stones may break my bones, but names will never hurt me" theory is that many of us tend to believe what others say about us because their words reinforce the same things that we say to ourselves. So in essence, it isn't what someone says, it is what we believe. It is also a result of being disconnected to the core of our being, which is love. This is when words begin to affect us.

If we don't give credence to what someone is saying, it won't impact us. Here is an extreme example. If someone calls you stupid but you have a 150 IQ and just walked out of a Mensa meeting, more than likely you will laugh it off. But it would be hard to ignore someone who was calling stupid if you did it to yourself numerous times a day because you didn't accept that you were smart or capable.

> Victory attained by violence is tantamount to a defeat, for it is momentary.
>
> —(Mahatma Gandhi, Indian leader and nonviolence activist)

There is another form of violence that we engage in when we communicate with others. It is something called blocking. We do this when we shut people down during verbal interactions. An example of this might be as simple as when our spouse tells us they want to go to the movies, and we respond by saying, "I don't want to." A friend can tell you that they think it is going to rain, and you respond with, "No, it isn't. I saw the weather report." It can be presented in more extreme forms such as someone telling us their hopes, wishes, and dreams, and we respond by saying something like "That's dumb. Why would you want to do that?" Or "That will never work."

Some of these examples may seem trivial or trite. However, it is important to remember that words have an enormous amount of power to hurt, belittle, and/or make people feel insignificant or inadequate. Moreover, ask yourself why you would want to hurt someone? More than likely, the answer is that we are hurting ourselves and don't know any other way to deflect the pain. However, we can always find a space of acceptance and kindness to interact with those around us. We just need to want to genuinely come to a place of understanding. Doing this would change responses like "That's dumb" to "Tell me more. I want to know why you feel that way." Or "I'd love to join you for a movie. Tonight doesn't work for me, but I'd love to find another time to go." Violence with words is one of the most prominent forms of viciousness in today's society. That is why it is important to be careful about what we say and how we interact with those who come into our reality.

> As the tongue speaketh to the ear so the gesture speaketh to the eye.
>
> —(King James the First, 1605)

It's More than Just a Finger

Another aspect of violence comes in the form of our gestures. Giving someone the finger or brushing your child away because you are too busy is violence. It is not necessary. It is not nice. And it doesn't do anything but make someone feel angry, upset, or unloved. Moreover, it can easily propagate more violence. The person you flipped off on the road may already have anger and violence issues. So your gesture may have fueled that person just enough to go home and beat their wife or child. Or out of frustration, ignoring your child may prompt them to abuse the family pet, a friend, or in the worst-case scenario, become the school bully. We never know how our actions or words will influence another. We must remember that there is nothing that anyone does that warrants any kind of abuse—period. When we mistreat and upset others, we are effectively hurting ourselves.

> We may never be strong enough to be entirely nonviolent in thought, word, and deed. But we must keep nonviolence as our goal and make strong progress towards it.
>
> —(Mahatma Gandhi, nonviolent political and spiritual leader of India)

How Is Nonviolence Related to Human Values?

Nonviolence is a worldview. It is the simple equation of cause and effect. Violence in actions, words, or deeds is the result of what happens when we don't have the other values in place. It is what happens when we extract the seed of love from our hearts. We must use love as the driving force behind all our values. Violence also festers in those who have little or no peace at their core. Without peace, life circumstances become exaggerated points in our mundane realities leading us to unrealistic viewpoints. Violence comes when we make poor choices as we end up angry with ourselves or look to blame others. Violence comes when there is no truth on our lips as living with a lie is like waiting to be sentenced for perjury. Violence is the results of our values getting lost and feeling like a ship with no harbor stuck in the middle of the ocean navigating a monumentous storm. It is the manifestation of hurt, pain, guilt, lonliness, and a lack of understanding for ourselves or others. So it is particularly important to be conscious and aware of what violence looks like through our words, gestures, and actions because love and violence cannot coexist in the same space. Our basic nature is nonviolent when we put the other values into practice.

> Nonviolence means avoiding not only external physical violence but also internal violence of spirit. You not only refuse to shoot a man, but you refuse to hate him.
>
> —(Martin Luther King Jr., American Baptist minister and civil rights leader)

What is violence?

We don't have to look very far to see the result of violence. Turn on a television, read a newspaper, or simply walk through the streets. It's everywhere. It's prevalent. It's consuming. It is destroying people, animals, and the planet. It is (unfortunately) on nearly every square meter of the globe. Violence is rampant in our thoughts, words, and actions. It is propagated at every turn. Violence is represented as viciousness against each other, foul language, television, excessive waste, clear-cutting the rainforests, domination for mining rights, human trafficking, illegal poaching, excessive meat consumption, and consumerism (to name only a few). It is the complete absence of love.

In turn, people and Mother Earth are responding in accordance to the energy that surrounds and infiltrates every cell of our being. This energy is radiating into the earth, and from this, death, destruction, and chaos ensues. The global devastation around the world is proof that our inner turmoil is turning itself outward. Violence has permeated the world. But it isn't who we are or the nature of our being.

I understand the effects of violence all too well. As I mentioned, I was brought up in an abusive household. The abuse connected on every level—physical, emotional, sexual, and neglect. As a child and even as a young woman, I had a lot of rage and anger built up inside me because I had not come to terms with my past and was unable to forgive my abusers. I felt that life and God owed me something and I became lost in the victim role of my life. To counter this, I masked the hurt and pain with an overzealous need to be perfect. Sometimes I would slip up, and my fury would lash out at someone or something. It came out as criticsm and judgment toward others. But most of the time, it was directed with hate and loathing toward myself. With so much turmoil and fire brewing inside, it is no wonder I didn't spontaneously combust.

> Ego stops you from getting things done and getting people to work with you. That's why I firmly believe that ego and success are not compatible.
>
> —(Harvey Mackay, businessman and columnist)

For a long time, my ego was in complete and total control of my life. And it moved through the world shouting, "The world owes me." So I spent most of my twenties and early thirties depressed and hopeless. Granted, I had some good moments as was not living as a complete train wreck. But in between the cracks, I would binge-drink, eat to numb myself, take advantage of people, and bully myself. As I mentioned, I had the potential to have a temper that I felt needed to be controlled. For the most part, I was able to do this. But my incessant fear that I would explode or someone would find out my secret kept me from living my life to the fullest. I felt I had to be contained because being transparent or vulnerable would be the kiss of death. I didn't know myself or what was really fueling my anger. I had no conscious connection to my inner divinity. But the truth was that I was so scared of finding out the answers and unraveling my true identity that I gave up on myself, people, and my dreams.

In my early years, this was also one of the primary reasons I gave myself for never wanting children. I was afraid of what I would do to them if I was capable of hurting myself with my own words and actions. The point is, violence is never the answer. Finding out what is at the core of your feelings and working through your pain can unleash your true potential.

> Because even the smallest of words can be the ones to hurt you, or save you.
>
> —(Natsuki Takaya, Japanese manga artist)

Words Hurt

As I reflect on my childhood, I no longer feel the sting of a slap, belt, or beating. But I remember the words that my parents said to me. I clearly remember their taunting and bullying. I also remember being told I was worthless and how they wished I was never born. Those words not only hurt me as a child, but carried into my relationships and life as an adult. Because the words were so ingrained, I unconsciously started to become the words that hurt me. This was the lingering effect of violence in my life. Although, I was no longer with the people who hurt me, the tapes played in my head on a continuously repeated cycle. Until I understood my patterns, I unknowingly remained the recipient of violence.

My story is far from unique. Abuse on some level is rampant in today's society. Bing.com defines abuse as "maltreatment: the physical, psychological, or sexual maltreatment of a person or animal." As a result of abuse, we are seeing more victimization, child suicides, and assaults on the rise. Murder has become the cornerstone of some cities. The problem has become so rampant that in an article written by Makini Brice (2102), he compare the city of Chicago to the war zone of Afghanistan. He said, "Since 2001, 1,976 Americans have died in Afghanistan. During that same period in time, 5,056 murders have taken place in Chicago."

Although the experts do not have any concrete answers as to why it is increasing, it doesn't need to be this way. But even though there is no empirical data to support why the world is perpetuating more violence, the answer cause is simple. We are devoid of love. However, we can learn to change our violent words, thoughts, and self-deprecating talk. We can put away our weapons. To help further curb our appetite for violence, we can stop watching violent television shows, movies, and engaging in violent games. Moreover, we can stop watching the news, which is nothing more than a daily recap of all the drama throughout the world. We can also stop telling ourselves that hitting and violence can be justified. We can move our hearts back into compassion and understanding.

People don't realize that violence is an energy that permeates our lives. We must do everything that we can to avoid seeing, hearing, or engaging in any kind of violence. By constantly assaulting our senses with the energy from violence, we start to become desensitized and somewhat immune to how it impacts us. We view ourselves as separate from each other, leaving us feeling vulnerable and exposed. As a result, we end up angry, bitter, scared, depressed, and/or volatile for sometimes inexplicable reasons.

Living abroad, I did not hear (or rarely heard) curse words. It isn't that people didn't say them. However, they had almost zero impact on me in another language as my brain did not make a connection. However, after returning to the States, I felt like I was being bombarded with every foul word in the book. On every corner, I heard people using harsh language in daily conversations and with each other. I felt that I was being verbally battered at every turn. This was and is auditory violence. Sadly, since I've now been back for some time, the words don't seemingly impact me as much because I'm used to them. But the truth still remains: inappropriate language is a violation to the senses just as much as bullying or other forms of verbal abuse. Over time, if we continue to surround ourselves with negative energy, it will move to meet the energy that surrounds us.

> Children will watch anything, and when a broadcaster uses crime and violence and other shoddy devices to monopolize a child's attention, it's worse than taking candy from a baby. It is taking precious time from the process of growing up.
>
> —(Newton N. Minow, American attorney and former chairman of the Federal Communications Commission)

Children and Violence

We can teach children and each other about how words hurt and the consequences of how our words can significantly influence an individual or the collective consciousness. We can teach children (and ourselves) that they are more than what others think about them. We can model appropriate interactions. We can show them how to use kind words to speak to others. We can refrain from using foul language in their presence. We can also teach them to walk away. We can practice love in its unconditional form, releasing ourselves and others from a constant battering of judgments. And if for some reason we can't find it within ourselves to love ourselves and everything around us, then we need to separate ourselves from the situation until we can find a space of neutrality. Otherwise, we can't effectively practice forgiveness and nonattachment toward the people who have caused us pain. Getting stuck in our emotions (our ego) is where violence begins. This is also not living life to our fullest. It is simply existing between the spaces of negative emotions.

> Forgiveness is a gift you give yourself.
> —(Suzanne Somers, American actress)

What Is Forgiveness?

In an article published by the world-famous Mayo Clinic website (2011), they said, "Forgiveness is a decision to let go of resentment and thoughts of revenge. The act that hurt or offended you might always remain a part of your life, but forgiveness can lessen its grip on you and help you focus on other, positive parts of your life. Forgiveness can even lead to feelings of understanding, empathy and compassion for the one who hurt you." It is also the only way to move forward and to open up your heart to begin the healing process.

> When you hold resentment toward another, you are bound to that person or condition by an emotional link that is stronger than steel. Forgiveness is the only way to dissolve that link and get free.
>
> —(Catherine Ponder, author and American minister for Unity Church)

My own experiences have taught me that closing off forgiveness is essentially allowing the person who hurt you to continue to have power over you. More simply put, the person who took your power or broke your spirit will continue to have control over you until you release them (forgive). As such, you allow them to continue to hurt you. Once you let go (forgive), you will be free, and your heart will once again open to love.

It never serves your highest good to hold on to old negative feelings toward anyone—including yourself. Learning to forgive ourselves is a key point that many people overlook because we tend to look at others when we indulge in the blame game. We must honestly assess our lives and take account for the part we play in the burden and hurt that we carry around on our shoulders. It only makes sense that if we can't find a space to absolve ourselves from mistakes, we will certainly struggle to truly forgive others for their transgressions.

Learn to forgive yourself. Learn to forgive others. Be free from the burden of negativity and hatred. It is the only way for you to truly be released from the past and be able to live freely with love in the present.

What Are the Benefits of Forgiving Someone?

Forgiveness is so essential to our positive evolution that the Mayo Clinic is even promoting its advantages. In an article on the Mayo Clinic website (2011), it suggests that "letting go of grudges and bitterness can make way for compassion, kindness and peace." Forgiveness can lead to the following:

- Healthier relationships
- Greater spiritual and psychological well-being
- Less anxiety, stress, and hostility
- Lower blood pressure
- Fewer symptoms of depression
- Lower risk of alcohol and substance abuse

> Sincere forgiveness isn't colored with expectations that the other person apologize or change. Don't worry whether or not they finally understand you. Love them and release them. Life feeds back truth to people in its own way and time.
>
> —(Sara Paddison, author)

What Is the Importance of Forgiveness?

This is such an important point that it bears repeating. Forgiveness is the only way forward. It is the one thing that will bring you the peace you need to move forward with your life. If we don't learn to truly forgive, then we become trapped in a battle between the ego and power struggles within and with other people. Forgiveness doesn't mean that we have to condone someone's behavior. And it certainly isn't permission for them to repeat the act. It is simply about letting go.

Forgiveness vs. the Ego

Sometimes, we find that it seems impossible to let go of our feelings toward someone who has wounded us. This happens when our ego takes on one of two very distinct roles when we are hurting or in pain: victim or perpetrator. In some cases, it even takes on both roles in a power struggle as highlighted in the following story.

I knew a man who was a great example of this dynamic. As a child, his mother was a drug abuser. As a result, she was neglectful in her duties as a mother. And his father was nowhere in the picture. As such, he turned all of his anger and hatred toward his mother. Later on in life, she found out that she was dying of cancer. She was trying everything to release her own anger and mend the relationship with her son. She understood the importance of forgiveness and wanted to heal the negative emotions and foster the best relationship that she could with her son in her last days. However, the man's ego said no. Not only was she dying, but her son was all she had in her last days.

As a result, he now had "power" over her to cause pain by denying her forgiveness, compassion, or understanding. However, at the same time, he continued to brew in his anger and resentment toward his mother, thereby taking on both roles of victim and perpetrator. He was lost in his childhood memories of what happened to him. He allowed the vicious cycle to continue to grow. He grew angrier and angrier with her as her health failed. He simply refused to forgive or acknowledge her humanness. At one point, I asked him if he could just look at her as a human being who was scared and dying—not as his mother. His answer was an emphatic no.

Sadly, she died before they could ever heal their pain. In the end, not only did he not make amends with his past, but the rage and resentment that he carried also destroyed some of his other relationships too. He lived his life unable to forgive his mother, himself, or other people for their humanness.

Forgiveness isn't always easy. It takes strength and courage. In my own life, I have had to do a lot of forgiving. Anyone who has heard some of the details of my past tends to ask me, "How is it possible that you don't hate these people?" The answer is that I love myself more than allowing my past to dictate my future. I am not giving anyone a hall pass. I have not forgotten what people have done. But I also realize that people who are damaged and in pain do things to harm and hurt others. Most people don't set out to make others miserable. They just do what they know, act out how they feel, or try to meet their needs at any cost. They don't love themselves or are afraid, so how are they expected to acting lovingly toward others? If I can't find a space to love and forgive others, I certainly won't find a place to love and forgive myself as we are all here in this life having a human experience, which means we are bound to make mistakes.

> Violence against one is violence against all. Violence against all is violence against myself.
> —(Charlie Crews, motivational speaker)

What Is It to Be a Victim?

As in the case of the man in the above story, he played the victim in the dynamic with his mother. He refused to take personal responsibility for his life as an adult. He lived in his story as the abused child. As victims, we need to maintain "our story" to feel validation for the crappy life or situations we are in. With time and without forgiveness, the role of the victim and the story become our identity. Once it becomes the identity, forgiveness becomes an abstract, unrelatable concept because we have integrated our role of victim into our psyche and moved it into an even deeper level—our molecular structure. Once it is integrated at the cellular level, we *are* the story. There is nothing that separates us from it anymore. Our thoughts become violent against ourselves. We degrade our worth and divinity. Ego quickly squashes any positive thoughts that dare enter our periphery. In essence, we declare war upon ourselves with a bombardment of negative self-talk and self-depredating ideologies. The ego tries to (and usually does) prevail in this battle at any cost.

> So many people prefer to live in drama because it's comfortable. It's like someone staying in a bad marriage or relationship—it's actually easier to stay because they know what to expect every day, versus leaving and not knowing what to expect.
>
> —(Ellen DeGeneres, American comedienne, actress, and television host)

Completely Lost in the Story

A friend of mine had a friend who became "her story." For many, many years, she was sick. As time went on, the pills and the ailments were all that she talked about. She also realized that it was a powerful hook to keep people's attention. But over time, she lost friends and family as no one wanted to hear her loop of complaints. She had been labeled as a hypochondriac by those who knew her. Over time, she became more ill. The problems kept building. The pain kept getting worse; try as they might, there was never a doctor who could ever really figure out what was troubling her. This went on for fifteen or so years until eventually, she became harmful to herself as she was not taking care of herself or her basic day-to-day needs. My friend stepped in to help. However, her efforts only continued to enable her story as it was giving her the attention she so desperately craved.

During the time my friend was assisting her, the woman had several surgeries in an attempt to correct the ailments. Each treatment and surgery was more promising. From an outside perspective, she should have been feeling like a million dollars. But once each surgery was complete, another problem magically cropped up. Nothing she did, pill she took, or remedy she tried worked for long. But it wasn't because she was sick per se; it was that the ideas and thoughts were now deeply embedded into every cell of her being. After fifteen years, she didn't know how to identify herself as anything but sick. The result was she actually "became" sick. But this was merely physical manifestations of emotional problems.

People like this woman tend to unconsciously believe that if they were to get better, all the care and concern from others would go away because they don't feel lovable or worthy. Without their story, they don't exist. This usually stems from old resentments and past issues that have not been addressed (usually related to childhood traumas). So they incorrectly mistake the attention they get from being ill for love and acceptance. As such, they, like this woman, end up stuck in and perpetuating a vicious, violent, unhealthy cycle of being a victim trapped in the prison of their lives. Once so deeply enmeshed, it is difficult to change such ingrained patterns. Yet, there is a simple solution and the process starts with love and forgiveness.

My Story

After writing the section above, I was listening to some wonderful inspirational, spiritual music by vocalist

Karen Drucker. The music is alive, powerful, and speaks to my soul. Later that day, I was taking my dogs for a walk. The wisdom of the music was still with me, so I was feeling very conscious and present. All of a sudden, I came to really understand something very important about the human condition: we *all* have a story. I knew this before, but it hadn't completely integrated on a personal level.

As I took a closer look at my own life, I realized that on any given day when someone had asked me or I asked myself, "How are you?" my ego typically wanted to complain about something. It wanted to feed off all the wrongs and betrayals that it had perceived not just that day, but for the first half of my life. It wanted to keep dredging up the past as if there wasn't anything else to discover. It was determined to make excuses for my bad behaviors or inappropriate reactions because at some point in my life, I had encountered some sort of abandonment, abuse, or neglect. My ego needed my story to live, or it would lose part of the definition of who I was. But that's just it—it is who I *was*. That was my past. It doesn't define who I am now. A story is just that, a story. I can decide when to move on to another chapter or just close the book. You can also proclaim, "This is not my life and I consciously choose another ending or the way I want my story written."

Simple Truth

What I have come to realize is that anything I did in my past (this includes yesterday) was when I didn't know how to do any better, nor did I have a clear understanding about who I am. If I could have done better, I would have done things better. I have never once set out to intentionally make myself or anyone else miserable. Every choice, thought, action, etc., was made based upon where I was in that moment of time. In addition, some of my past was at a time when I was in relationships with some people who also didn't know better and were doing the best they could too. It was a time before I remembered or even conceptually knew that I was divine love and a perfect manifestation of God. It was before I was completely conscious. This is a point to remember for yourself and others. In fact, no one wakes up with a diabolical plan to destroy themselves and everyone around them. If they do, it is because they have completely lost the face of God.

So even though my story hadn't made me physically ill, it had made me mentally sick as my mind and body were nearly always on some level (however minute) in a constant state of stress, fear, or worry. I could pretend for some time that my high self had slayed the ferocious beast (my ego), but it tended to be a short-term victory as I quickly came to realize that there was more than one head to cut off the monster! Since I am still (as we all are) in a learning curve, I can pretty much guarantee that I will make mistakes from time to time. But now, I won't wallow (for long). I will simple forgive myself, turn the page, or close the book for a while. But the challenge is to make sure that you never let the moment go without making an effort to understand the lesson the universe was trying to teach you. At the core of every life lesson is an opportunity to move yourself back toward love.

What Is It to Be the Perpetrator?

Earlier in the book, I talked a little bit about being a victim. But in essence, being a victim and a perpetrator are essentially the same role. In fact, there is a very fine line that separates the two. However, the perpetrator tends to feed off the power taken by victimizing others. The power feeds the ego, and the ego (greedy in nature) requires more and more to survive. The cycle becomes a never-ending loop.

> Hitler and Gandhi were both able-minded, but the later was also noble-hearted. That's the difference.
>
> —(Author unknown)

Where Is the Fine Line?

The fine line is that most perpetrators are living in fear. In essence, they are the "victims" of themselves, their thoughts, deeds, and actions.

During my seven years of traveling the globe, I worked at a private school in the United Arab Emirates as a human values instructor. I was hired by the director to incorporate human values into the classroom and develop the program. Ironically, the director of the school was terribly unkind and would harshly and inappropriately speak to his staff members. He was also extremely stingy with his money. He ran the school like a business, not a center for educating young, vulnerable minds. As a result, there was a high turnover rate with the staff, and the school had a very bad reputation.

His value structure and what he was asking me to teach were in direct conflict. So I left the position. What I was told later was that he had a lot of personal financial trouble with his outside investments. He was also a proud man and seemed to want status and recognition for who he was. As a result, his fear of losing money and status propagated his role of perpetrator. In turn, the perpetrator had become the victim of his own ego.

Each role (victim or perpetrator) leads to self-destruction. Ultimately, this is violence either toward the self or others. Then once we are within the violence, it is only natural to look for outlets to express our feelings and to release the anger, fear, sadness, and ego-driven desires. Eventually, because the ego becomes so overdeveloped, it has only one goal: to be right at any cost. So without all the other values in alignment, we forget about love and forgiveness being the precursors to peace and happiness. In the end, we approach life in the way of "I'd rather be right than happy."

Confirmation Bias

In psychology, this can be likened to the concept of confirmation bias, which is the tendency to look for and favor information that confirms one's thoughts, beliefs, and/or actions. So essentially, to maintain our "rightness," we use any measure necessary—text, religious doctrine, excuses, our own reasons, or the reasoning of others—all in the quest to support our ego. The results of these efforts can be innumerous, contributing to everything from pain to sadness, destruction, drug abuse, or even death. The only way to counter violence is to change the thoughts, practices, and to live immersed in all the values. And most importantly, we must forgive in the most complete and unconditional sense of the word.

After a friend's divorce, she insisted that she had forgiven her ex-husband. Yet everything she did and said was to the contrary of the concept of forgiveness. She would look to anyone and any circumstance that would confirm her feelings about him and his behavior. As such, she continued to hold on to an excessive amount of bitterness and anger toward him. She would verbalize the words "I forgive him" and then make one hundred excuses why her children could not see their no-good father. These are obviously contradicting thoughts as well as actions. Furthermore, they are clearly not in the realm of forgiveness. Again, the only way forward in the quest toward love and nonviolence is forgiveness.

> Nobody can go back and start a new beginning, but anyone can start today and make a new ending.
>
> —(Maria Robinson, fiction writer)

Is It Possible to Change?

Change is very possible. It is also not an easy road to traverse because it requires taking personal responsibility for our own lives, our choices, our ailments, words, actions, and our thoughts. There is no more blame or wallowing allowed in the movement from victim (or perpetrator) to empowered God-self. Change is a road less traveled, but a remarkably rewarding journey to take. It moves you from who you think you are, and others perceive you to be to who you really are at your essence—a divine being.

> Spanking is simply another form of terrorism. It teaches the victims that might makes right, and that problems can be solved through the use of violence by the strong against the weak.
>
> —(Anonymous)

Hitting Is Never the Answer

Physical punishment is clearly violence. Hitting and screaming are never the answers. Physical abuse is degrading for anyone. But specifically, it teaches children that violence is a resolve to get what we want. It also teaches your children to obey you out of fear and not out of respect or love. Parents hit because they are frustrated and want immediate results from their children. Physical (otherwise known as corporal) punishment has immense potential to destroy the relationship between a parent and child as it can "evoke feelings of fear, anxiety, and anger in children" (Gershoff, 2002). Studies have also shown that corporal punishment can lead to "a number of behavioral problems and antisocial behavior in childhood, adolescence and adulthood because of its link with physical maltreatment and abuse potential in some families" (University of North Carolina School of Medicine, 2010). In the simplest terms, physical and mental abuse is violence, and violence begets violence. Abuse is reacting without love. It inflicts pain and shame. And it can't be rationalize any other way.

I am not for a second suggesting that parenting is easy. But I am going to go out on a limb here and say, "If you don't have the time or patience to be a parent, don't have children." Children deserve your time and attention. Children are in your care to be guided, loved, nurtured, and taught. They are not yours to abuse, neglect, or dismiss.

So How Do I Handle It?

Although I am not a parent, I completely understand the frustration around trying to get immediate results. I have been a substitute and/or regular staff teacher for over thirteen years. I have taught every age, from preschool to university. As such, I know firsthand that maintaining an orderly learning environment can be a challenge within itself. I understand that unruly behavior can be a minute-by-minute challenge in trying not to lose it. I also understand that children act out for a reason. And if we can get to the root of problem, we can move to restore peace and order with love.

As I have mentioned, I am the proud parent of a puppy. Lia is, without question, a joy in my life. She is also an energetic and at times rather vocal handful. Several dog trainers have diagnosed as hyperactive and assertive. In more simplistic terms, she thinks she is in charge.

When I lived in Korea, I had to get up rather early to care for her and my much older dog named Belleza before getting myself off to work. During this time, I lived in about a hundred-square-foot apartment that wasn't known for its soundproof features. Every morning without fail, as soon as I stepped into the shower, Lia took it as her cue to antagonize Belleza. Belleza is normally incredibly quiet and very sweet in nature. But as things are in the animal kingdom, she didn't take kindly to a young pup getting in her face. As such, this battle of wills and dominance always ended up in a loud barking match around 6:00 a.m. Of course, this is *not* neighbor-friendly behavior even under the best of conditions. As a result, a typical shower lasted about sixty seconds as I would have to jump out and quiet the dogs.

> Violence is not power—it is the absence of power.
>
> —(Author unknown)

Puppy Parenting 101

One morning, I was particularly tired and wanted to have my shower in peace and quiet. However, on cue, Lia started antagonizing Belleza. I tried shouting through clenched teeth in an attempt to sound angry without the volume. But that clearly didn't work. The barking ensued and was getting louder and louder. I was so angry that I jumped out of the shower, nearly fell on the wet floor (making me more upset), and reached for Lia to swat her on the butt to quiet her. Fortunately, she is quick and didn't get much of my hand. But just as soon as I touched her, I realized that I had let the values escape me. In my quest for silence and control, I had lost my sense of inner peace and embarked upon a path of violence. I could have really hurt her as at the time, she was all of a teeny, tiny three pounds total in size. But more than that, I don't want her to obey me out of fear. I want her to do it from a place of love and with as much understanding as we can communicate to each other.

Children need the same consideration, time, and attention. They need to understand what they are doing wrong with nonviolent communication practices (see helpful resources page). If at anytime you feel that you have to hit someone or an animal, you are doing something wrong—not the other way around.

> We have enslaved the rest of the animal creation, and have treated our distant cousins in fur and feathers so badly that beyond doubt, if they were able to formulate a religion, they would depict the Devil in human form.
>
> —(William Ralph Inge,
> Outspoken Essays, 1922)

What Is Violence Against Nature?

The third greatest atrocity is violence against nature. People fail to realize that unnecessary consumerism, excessive meat consumption, not recycling, littering, wasting food, misusing resources, etc., are all violence against the planet. Yet some people are oblivious to the carbon footprint that they are leaving on the earth. And in many cases, they flat out don't care about the damage that they are doing, stating, "The whole global warming issue is a big conspiracy theory or entirely overexaggerated." Or they simply say, "I am only one person. What can I do about it?" I say it only took one man to free India from British tyranny. If Gandhi had the strength and fortitude as one man in an impoverished condition, we too individually can make changes to perpetuate nonviolence on a personal and global level. It doesn't take much to recycle or simply purchase a reusable water bottle.

During my last year in Korea, I was in a Starbucks waiting for my chai tea to arrive. While I was waiting, a woman started talking to her boyfriend. She said, "Starbucks should encourage people to bring their own cups. If they do, they should give them a discount on their beverage. That would sure make the tree huggers happy." She then completed her statement with "But I'd never do it, even if they offered it." Just then my tea arrived in my own personal tumbler, and I gave her a proud tree-hugging smile.

Starbucks did all the things that she was suggesting. But more than that, her final comment was a great example of how people make great Monday morning planetary quarterbacks, but just can't seem to be bothered or care enough to help the earth on even the smallest scale. I guess if I would have been a little more courageous, I would have asked her, "Why wouldn't you bring your own beverage container? It is simple, cost-effective, and saves trees."

Right conduct and nonviolence, in many cases, go hand in hand with each other as cooperative principles. When we make choices with conscientious awareness, we can avoid violent acts against nature, others, and ourselves. If we truly want to help others, ourselves, and the planet, we must start from within and act in accordance with our beliefs for transformation. As Gandhi once said, "Be the change you wish to see."

The All-Pervading Ego

Self-importance is man's greatest enemy. What weakens him is feeling offended by the deeds and misdeeds of his fellow men. Self-importance requires that one spend most of one's life offended by something or someone.

—(Don Juan, legendary fictional libertine)

The Power of the Ego

When it comes to fully embracing the values, the ego can be your biggest adversary. It is easy to be fooled as the ego is very tricky and deceptive. If you try to ignore it, it will make every effort to look for someone or something to feed it. It is tenacious and will stop at nothing to be indulged. One of the best examples of this feeding frenzy is within our relationships.

When we are getting to know someone (which can take a lifetime), we make an extraordinary effort to put our best face forward. We (our egos) may start out our time together, talking or thinking about our fears and failures as if they are markers of who we are and where we came from. In some cases, we may even view them as badges of honor. Then we wait for compliments and praise as approval of our personal self-worth as defined by our hardships. We may even fall into old patterns that create a blockage to opening our hearts to the other person. We may even judge a person with the measuring stick we used from our past relationships. Conversely, some of us make every effort to become what we think the other person is looking for in a potential partner. In some cases, we talk about our life accomplishments to help define our personal and worldly value. But in most cases, consciously or unconsciously, we tend to revisit some drama or an aspect of our false self that comes from the past. This is our ego vying for attention.

Either way, in those beginning stages, we place a great amount of value on what the other person thinks of us. Sometimes we use stories about our lives as competitions for whose life, divorce, breakup, job, day, etc., is or was worse. Other times, we start to keenly watch their every move to see if they will be a recreation of the past. Or we move through the relationship blindly as our need for love is so intense that we mistake it for lust and attachment. To add to this, if our ego is not fed just the right amount of information or compliments to adequately satiate its hunger, eventually it decides to judge, label, and criticize ourselves and those around us. When this consistently happens, we become hurt or feel rejected.

At the end of all this mind chatter and emotional confusion, it is only the ego that wins out as it gets to keep the story of my life. Although most of us are well-intentioned, we rarely get too far into relationship with the idea that we are going to love the other unconditionally and allow them to be exactly who they are without judgment or faith that one day they will change some behavior. Of course, we all want that to be our reality. We hope that is how it will work out for us, but the false self usually prevails and moves toward heart-closing behaviors.

As a general rule, the ego would rather be right than happy. Right leaves us feeling full and satisfied, but only for a short time as the ego will rise to be fed again. The ego always wants to feel important. It wants to feel certainty and significance. It also wants connection and some variety. The ego keeps us stuck in antiquated belief patterns about ourselves and in judgment of others. The ego keeps us on the highs and lows of self-worth and satisfaction. But we are so much more than our limited perspectives. God doesn't make junk (the halo benders). So this cyclical reality that we put ourselves in also happens to be the farthest thing from our right to happiness and our true nature—our inner divinity that is pure love, God. Moreover, we must stop to think about what is really important and ask ourselves if the battles we chose to fight have any merit or are we just sparring to win. If you think about it, how critical is it that the cap is off the toothpaste, yet again? Is it a topic worth losing your focus of love?

I have been teaching nearly every genre of psychology online for over ten years at the university level. So I have very academic understanding of how human beings work and how the ego comes into play. One of the most famous descriptions of the ego comes from Freud. He discussed the ego in three different parts: id, ego, and super ego. In simplest terms, the id is our pleasure principle. It wants immediate gratification at all costs. The ego is based on the reality principle. It works to please the id in realistic and socially appropriate ways. The super ego is probably the most valuable for working with human values as it wants to live by a code of standards. It helps us discern between right and wrong. But it can also want to please those who it deems an authority figure. The paradox is that these three components are usually battling each other within us, which keeps our lives complicated. Rarely are people able to keep a balance. So these various aspects end up keeping us from truly imbibing the values as each part is struggling to try to maintain its position.

From a spiritual perspective, the belief is that the ego needs to be eradicated at all costs as it only serves us at a very mundane, rudimentary level. Therefore, it keeps us from discovering our true essence, which is that of God. This is the goal of the spiritual aspirant. But the truth is that we just need to consistently live in love. It is impossible for the ego to share the same space as divine love. So we don't need to fight the ego. We just need to be blissfully happy with love at our forefront directing us to our true North. This is the ultimate goal of human values.

> It is not worth losing your smile for anything out there.
>
> —(Sri Sri Ravi Shankar, spiritual leader, proponent for nonviolence and the founder of the Art of Living)

Welcome to the Club

Here's the thing that you need to set straight with your ego: even if you had or have a difficult life (which most of us have), those experiences have led you to who and where you are today. In 2005, Steve Jobs (Apple and Pixar CEO) said in a commencement speech at Stanford University, "You can't connect the dots looking forward. You can only connect them looking backwards. So you have to trust that the dots will somehow connect in your future. You have to trust in something—your gut, destiny, life, karma, whatever." He was correct. When most people hear that speech, their innate wisdom wholly agrees. However, when we go out into the world, our ego works overtime to keep us trapped in self-centered realities. The ego does not want you to live in the values because over time, it knows that it will weaken and eventually cease to exist. The ego doesn't want to love from an unconditional space or foster forgiveness. It wants to judge, label, and feed off of self-righteousness.

Which Path Will You Choose?

Think of life as something like an old discovery map. You log where you've been, you see where you failed, and you remember the best routes to use should you have to navigate certain courses in the future. But you don't stop traveling just because you've been to a few places. You keep learning and steering through the journey of your life. Depending upon presenting circumstances, in the moment, you may not be able to see the value of your past or even present because you may be in the dead center of a terrible storm. This happens. And even though the storm may leave a trail of destruction in its wake, in time, this too shall pass. No matter what the experience, you will come out the other side just a little bit or a whole lot wiser than when everything started. You don't stop discovering because you get a little lost or had a bad experience. These are only temporary hiccups on the road of life. This is why it is so important not to let the ego take a hold and run away with you. This is why the values are so indispensable. Every step of the way is an opportunity where you can learn and grow or stagnate and wither. It is your choice to be a victim of the past or a positive cocreator with the divine in this present moment. It is a chance for you to open your heart and learn more about love.

Unreality TV

Without a doubt, having a sad or destructive story is a very quick way to get attention—just watch the news or open a newspaper. The fact is that it isn't the right kind of attention. It doesn't highlight our true worth or our inner divinity. Yet today, the media glorifies villains and offers fifteen minutes of fame to anyone noteworthy. We have a whole slew of "celebrities" who are only famous for being drunk, lascivious, lewd, obnoxious, immoral, ignorant, etc. Generally, these people are greatly rewarded for their dramatic stories and their poor behavior. It seems that the more drama there is, the higher the ratings. A perfect example of this is now what we call reality television. My question would be, "As a society, why are we allowing inappropriate conduct to be considered reality?"

According to the current trend in our society, to gain any kind of attention or notoriety, you must partake in negative, attention-seeking behaviors. These days it is a sure-fire way to climb the ladder of success. I could list a slew of "celebrities" who have come to be famous for sex tapes, drunken escapades, fights, etc. I can list another host of people who the public is intrigued with simply because of their poor choices. As a culture, we need to recontruct how we are going to start defining "normal" human behavior? We need to move to a space good values are the focus of our realities.

To the delight of the ego, this is a confusing message for the masses. On one hand, certain arenas of our lives are trying to keep us immersed in morality, while the rest of society is telling us that it is okay to live without a code of ethics or partaking in loving behaviors. In addition, people get a strange sense of satisfaction watching someone fail or falter. It becomes like a fight where the probabilities are 1 (morality) against 1,000 (ego). Those aren't good betting odds. Heck, even the battle between David and Goliath was one on one.

Don't Feed the Drama Beast

When you go to the zoo, there is a sign that says "Don't feed the monkeys." Like that sign, I too remind you, "Don't feed the drama beast!" When we engage in and support negative behaviors, it will only perpetuate an unhealthy lifestyle, stress, depression, and disease.

The Values Working Together

> True knowledge consists of understanding the unity that underlies the cosmos. All suffering and problems in life arise from the sense of duality.
>
> —(Sathya Sai Baba, Indian guru, spiritual figure, and educator)

Even though five separate values have been described, they ultimately work together as one. You cannot proceed faithfully or accurately with one value and not the others. It would be foolish to think that you can live in unconditional love and not be impeccable with your words. It is not any more possible than driving a car without some fueling component like electricity, oil, or gasoline. Everything must be as one unit to effectively work to raise our vibration and bring us to our innate inner divinity.

There is a rhythm, a balance, a universal dance that must take place. So when we don't move through the world with unconditional love and positive regard for all, we are not operating from a space of divinity—the place of "I am" divine love. When we do not plant the seed of love, root ourselves in love, and live in love, we forget our inner divinity. We move against our truth as we are not being honest with ourselves or others. This is not living in alignment with our thoughts, words, and actions. When this happens, we become out of balance. Thereby, the imbalance perpetuates unrest at our core (peace). When we are not centered (peace), we are unable to make good life-affirming choices that positively impact us and everything around us (right conduct). And when we aren't making good choices and things seem to continually go wrong, we get angry with ourselves and others (nonviolence). As a result, we tend to act out with unkind words or actions because we have forgotten love and forgiveness. These patterns, habits, and ways to negotiate our lives put us on a never-ending negative loop. This is why it is crucial to use all the individual values as one.

Derailed

In this day and age, it seems that it is terribly easy to get derailed from the authentic goodness that lies within each of us. Sometimes, we tend to just go as the wind blows us. Granted, living in the moment or going as the way opens is an excellent way to live *if* it is done with the concepts of love, nonattachment, and surrender at the forefront of our understanding. In other words, we must be sincerely unattached to the outcome of the day-to-day workings of our lives. This also means living with the values, in the present moment, and having complete faith in the divine.

Conversely, when we move with fear as our primary motivation, we can quickly lose the plot of our own existence and become enmeshed in other people's lives and value structures. In other terms, we take on their signatures. This is what typically happens to many of us. We become the company we keep. It is as the old adage states, "Water seeks its own level."

Take heed as to who your friends are and what kind of individuals you are spending time with on a daily basis. Decide who you want to be and how you can become a better version of yourself. Then, surround yourself with people who hold a higher moral standard and you will naturally excel to meet their level. In making these kinds of choices, you may lose people from your inner circle. As we grow and change for the better, we can't hold on to those who are no longer in alignment with our goals. In the long run, those people will start to feel like a ball and chain weighing you down and prohiniting you from moving forward.

When we continue to surround ourselves with those who do not meet or exceed our vibration, we can stop the stream of the goodness that we deserve, and we end up fighting against the natural flow of life. We try to push ourselves into worlds, onto people, and into situations that are not for our highest good. In the end, we are simply unhappy, discontent, or worse, we become complacent. If you think spending time with people who lie, cheat, steal, do drugs, or are morally corrupt won't have an impact on you, think again. Even the strongest of minds will be challenged to keep themselves in alignment with the values and their moral structure when we are continuously surrounded by negativity or discord.

> "Without credible communication, and a lot of it, the hearts and minds of others are never captured."
>
> —(John P. Kotter, Author and American Professor)

But She Said…

While living in the UAE, I met a woman who was so fickle you could (with the right words) convince her of nearly anything. For the time that I knew her, she had wanted to get into the fashion industry. All she talked about was the latest trends, collections, designers, etc. She had clear enthusiasm for the business. When I met her, she was a teacher who didn't like her job. After many hours of talking to her, she decided with great conviction and satisfaction that she was going to go back to school to pursue her long-time dream. She knew at her core that it was the right decision. For once, she seemed at peace and excited about her future. However, underlying every fiber of her being was fear.

One day I saw her, and she said, "You're going to be angry with me. I have decided to open a tutoring school. I met with a lady yesterday, and she said I should only do 'what I know.' And all I know is teaching." I could not believe my ears. First, it wasn't my place to be angry with her. So what she was really saying to me was "I *am* angry about not honoring my innate truth." Second, she was originally so resolute in her decision to pursue her vision in the fashion industry, yet after only one breakfast, she let someone convince her to go against her inner knowing and lifetime dream. I spoke to her again for about fifteen minutes, only to remind her of what she had said to me about her lack of desire to teach and her real passion.

Once again, she changed her mind and was determined to move forward with her goal. After I moved, we lost contact with one another. The last I heard, she had come up with another excuse not to follow her dream. But if I had to make a guess, she probably will never end up pursuing her goals simply because she cannot find the strength or fortitude within to release her fear of change or attachment to what others think or her inability to surrender to the flow of life. She easily got derailed from her inner guidance and wasn't willing to release impending fear and replace it with trust in her divine self. But more than that, she wasn't surrounding herself with people who believed in the flow of life and would support her dreams with unconditional love and acceptance. We may not always agree with what someone wants to do, but we have no business trying to to alter one's journey when our own paths have yet to be cleared.

Put your future in good hands—your own.
—(Author unknown)

A dear friend of mine had a dream to move to the United States to live the American dream. It was something that he wanted to do for as long as he could remember. One day, he e-mailed me to tell me that he was finally going to put in the paperwork and make his way to the States. I could feel the happiness and enthusiasm through the e-mail. He had everything planned out—how he would ship his belongings, who he would stay with once he arrived, etc. He was ready to fulfill a lifelong dream. It wasn't but a month later that he abandoned all his plans. He said the idea was too uncertain, and many people told him that he was foolishly risking everything. They said they themselves would not even consider such an uncertain venture. In the end, he bought into the uncertainty of those around him and could not trust that God and the God within would take care of everything if he would just allow. He let the power of fear and the doubts that other people had in their own minds and from their own limited experiences take away his happiness and dream.

Sadly, he had a history of things not working out as planned. As such, it wasn't a huge leap for him to believe others who shared his same need for certainty. If he could have faced his fears and learned to trust and surrender, he may be living a different life. The universe will guide us if we allow life to flow. But there are people who build massive dams to impede or self-sabotage their happiness. And they can do that simply by asking someone else what they think.

Blessed

After I returned to the States, I eventually landed in Chicago. About three months after I arrived, I met a wonderful woman (who was also new to Chicago) at the local dog park. At some point, she was telling me about how she came to live in Chicago. She is a very talented artist who wanted to sell her work on a larger scale. She had outgrown her life and her network where she had been living. So Chicago felt like the next step for her.

However, painting was her only income, and at the time, it wasn't bringing in the kind of money that would allow her to make the transition. So one night, she prayed to God and said, "If you want me to move to Chicago and it is your will, I need about $60,000." She let go of the outcome and trusted that God (her inner divinity) would direct her. She felt that if the move was meant to be, the way would open for her. However, in the meantime, she didn't ask a million people what they thought or if they thought she should make such a radical life change. She didn't fret or worry; she left it in God's hands. The move was in the divine plan and within a month, she had record sales for her art. People started coming to her house, knocking down her door, asking for her paintings. She made $60,000. From there, she prayed and said, "God, if still you want me to move, I am going to need a place to live in

Chicago." As it turned out, a friend of a friend had an open apartment. She offered her the apartment rent-free for three months while she looked for a permanent residence. Again, she continued to pray and trust. As she surrendered herself to the will of the divine, doors and opportunities easily opened and presented her with everything she needed. This story could have had a completely different outcome if she would have relied on the opinions and limiting beliefs of those around her.

This woman is an example of how we need to trust and surrender to the divine. But more than that, she is a lovely human being who naturally works to immerse herself in the values. She followed her heart and allowed God to be her driver, not those around her who could only offer her their limited perspective.

Sadly, many of us tend to become or do what others want. We do things, make choices, and believe based on what others expect from us, and rarely do we stop to question, "Why?" In essence, we end up living other people's lives and forget that we have our own path. Like in the example of my friend who wanted to move to the States, fear moves us, bending and throwing us about in and out of other people's paths and life stories. Then once we are so far out to sea, lost, alone, and fearful for our very existence to survive, we finally cry for help. But all the help we ever need is within us. To heal the pain and release the never-ending unhappiness, we must steep ourselves in human values. We must trust and surrender to the divine. We must have more faith in our abilities. We must immerse ourselves in love. We must believe! We must go back to the basics.

Going Back to the Basics

> Let no one suffer the slightest pain as a result of your thoughts, words, or deeds.
>
> —Sathya Sai Baba (Indian guru, spiritual figure, and educator)

The essence of every single person on this planet is God. If you prefer not to use the term God, then you can define this as you wish. One may think of it as a creative energy, a profound oneness with spirit, or whatever. However you define it, that fundamental nature is perfect, and it encompasses all of the five human values. It isn't something that some of us have and others don't. Even the most wicked person on the planet has a seed of goodness buried beneath a mountain of fear. To highlight this point, it was said that "Hitler cried profusely when his canary died" (the Nizkor Project). He was also a vegetarian. All we need to do is excavate through what we believe to be our mundane 3-D reality to find our true innermost being. The thing is that this is hardly an easy task. It takes love, courage, fortitude, tenacity, and strength of character to unearth our deepest, darkest fears and the truth of who we are—the essence of God (I am).

Personal Disasters = Blessings

I can't begin to count how many times my heart has been broken or my foundation unearthed. Each time, the pain seemed like it would consume me. There were even times where I was sure that I would never recover. There were other times I did not want to recuperate. I had lost all hope or will to continue on. But I did. I always found the strength to consciously or unconsciously remember that tomorrow is a new day. Nothing is forever. And whatever obstancle is in front of me will eventually pass. This wasn't always easy ground to traverse. But I managed to find a way through even in my darkest days.

Now when life throws me a curveball, the pain still comes. It takes a minute or a day, but I now recognize it is my ego crying out for attention. Nothing is ever as bad as it seems. But it is the inner turmoil and lack of peace that wants to make things bigger than what the situation deserves. It is getting side tracked from love and keeping fear as my compass point. However, when I remain submerged in the values, I tend to have a quicker rebound time from my personal "dramas" since I have come to realize that everything in my world that happens to me is for my highest good and that there is nothing around me but love if I remain open to it. I am not suggesting for a minute that I get to that place immediately or that it's easy. This awareness comes with patience and a lot of practice and, as I mentioned earlier, lots of pop quizzes from the universe. Like everyone else, I am still on a learning curve. My hope is that one day, there will be a time when I completely come to trust and surrender to my destiny (God's will) in the same amount of time that it takes me to blink my eyes.

As for all the personal disasters, well, those just led me to where I am today. They made me stronger, wiser, and more connected to my original nature. Ultimately, they all lent to teaching me the true nature of love. Therefore, there are no accidents or mistakes in my life. As such, I have no regrets. Everything that I have perceived as good or bad have been for my highest good. Honestly, when I look back at some of those heartbreaks, I get on my knees to thank God that I did not get what I asked for. None of the people I thought were good for me were even close to being what I needed for much more than a temporary insight and redirection back to myself and love. Now when people ask me what I want, I frequently repeat a joke I once heard: "How do you make God laugh? Tell him your plans!" I have come to realize that, truth be told, most of the time, I have no earthly idea what would be in my best interest. I can presuppose, guess, or even cajole, but if the past is any indication of my forecasting abilities, I'm not completely qualified to "plan my life." So now, I find it is just best to leave it to the divine design and say, "Thank you" for whatever comes my way.

So the next time a date doesn't return your call, you get stood up, don't get that job promotion, or something else doesn't go your way, know, truly understand that what doesn't come to fruition wasn't meant to be. In addition, you should also look at what you contributed to the situation. It is importatnt to remember that, you need to reflect on what you bring to the table in any dynamic and make the changes accordingly. Ask yourself what you need to learn from the lesson. Be introspective. Sometimes, someone or something that is presented to you is merely a tool to help you work through an unresolved issue and move you through to your next level of evolution or to remind you to move back into your heart space with love. Most importantly, no matter what the outcome, trust that God knows what is best for you.

> The only source of knowledge is experience.
>
> —(Albert Einstein)

Tragedy: The Precursor to Growth

So now we go back to the beginning, and I repeat some of the words that have been given to me over and over during my life. "From the greatest tragedies comes an immense amount of growth." Naturally, in the moment of our hurt, we tend to feel that we are suffering alone and that the intensity of our pain will never end. Yet as I shared, one day, it does end. Intuitively we know this because we've all had some reference or personal experience that has shown us that eventually the discomfort ends. As such, it is then our choice to continue the story or to simply practice love and forgiveness while reviewing the experience as an opportunity, a stepping stone, or a new direction to move through our lives. Where one door closes, a window opens. It is our choice to look for the opening or feel trapped because the door is closed. Life is simply perspective. William Shakespeare once said, “Nothing is either good or bad. It is the mind that thinks it is so.”

As I shared, from the beginning of my life up until this point, I have had some pretty hard knocks. Each time I got pushed down, trampled, battered, abused, and run over by life, I, as everyone does, have always had the choice to stay down or get up. I have had the choice to believe that there are good people in the world. I have had the choice to believe that I was worthy of love, and I would find love in my life and in everything around me. I had the choice to know that I was not my fears. I have had the choice to understand that I am more than just this vehicle I define as a body. I have had the choice to believe that today is the first day of the rest of my life. Conversely, I have always had the choice to quit too. It becomes simply about looking for the opening in the window or feeling trapped because the door has closed.

The point is that my choices are no different than anyone else’s. But each time life delivers a knee-buckling blow, we have to get up, dust off, and keep moving. Through the values, we can find our strength, will, and power to make the decisions that support our highest divine potential. Then trust and surrender knowing that no matter the ending, it was right in that moment. That is true courage.

> You have about as much free will as a donkey tied to a post.
>
> —(Sathya Sai Baba, Indian guru, spiritual figure, and educator)

Is This All Luck or Destiny?

Depending upon what one believes, there are many ways to qualify life. Some say that life is luck. Others believe that we just need to use positive thinking and affirmations to make our way through the world. In many ways, I think that life is already mapped out for us. But whether you go to work as a garbage man, a teacher, or as an executive, we all have the freedom (free will) to decide how we are going to do those jobs. Are you going to do them with love in your heart, steadiness at your core, and truth on your lips? Or are you going to build up more negative karma and ignore your inner divinity that is marked by the five human values?

> You can't change your destiny, but you can always change your mind.
>
> —(Milan Marie Hollister, author)

What Is Free Will?

I believe that fundamentally, the only real free will that we have on any given day is deciding how we are going to leave our signatures, our marks, our carbon footprints on every single person and thing that we come in contact with throughout that day. More simply put, it is how you respond to the daily happenings in your life. Are you freaking out, pissed off, devastated, and/or hopeless? Or is your inner peace so strong that it is like a repellent force field that allows nothing to penetrate your inner calm?

Through the basic human values, we can easily and successfully navigate life using these innate tools bestowed upon us by the divine. Again, it is a simple recipe for success. Yet many of us look for extreme, radical answers to sort out our lives. We attend workshop after workshop, lecture after lecture, and read book after book. Stop! Look within for what is already the essence of you: love, peace, truth, right conduct, and nonviolence. The divine infused us with these values to live healthy, happy, harmonious lives. This sentence bears repeating: the values are gifts given to us to successfully steer our existence, not just an accident that we were possibly meant to stumble upon at some point in the journey we call life.

Moreover, these treasures need to be passed down to our children at a very early age so that they can reap the benefits of their powerful, distinctive capabilities. Then little by little, child by child, the world will change for the better because we haven't allowed the children to stagger around, blindly searching for what they already possess.

I have heard so many parents talk about their concern related to not providing enough money for their child's future. They stress and fret over their children not having a big-enough college fund or inheritance for when they pass from this existence. But I say it isn't a parent's primary job to leave money or to focus on the mundane. That is the wrong kind of support. In fact, it would be far more productive if a parent could teach the children the value of education and saving money for themselves. Parents need to infuse their children with love and teach them that "The Wealth Within You, Your Essence, Is Your Kingdom" (Rumi) and imparting love on everyone no matter what is true strength of character. This would be far more effective in reinforcing the values. Children who learn, understand, and practice these values will grow up to be loving, fruitful adults. They will have the best tools possible to successfully pilot their lives and find fulfilling existences. That isn't something money can provide. Money comes and goes, but good values grow and grow. Think about how you view the world and if your vantage point is the most clear and untainted by worldy objective. Then remember that you are the sum of all your choices.

> Between stimulus and response there is space...
> In that space is our power to choose our response.
> In our response lies our growth and our freedom.
> —(Viktor Frankl, Auschwitz survivor)

How Do We Get Back?

Imagine our world if children grew up understanding and practicing the core key, basic human values. Imagine a world where adults practiced these values and emulated them for children. Imagine a world where pain and suffering were mere folktales told to remind us of what life was like without the values. Imagine your life content and with abounding love. This is all possible. It just takes a seed…one seed. Start out by planting the divine seed of unconditional love, and you will find that all of the other values will come a lot more easily to you. Make your journey through life easier. Go back to the basics and imbibe the human values—love, truth, peace, right conduct, and nonviolence.

How Do I Do That?

The first step in this process is love…love…love… love! To practice love, we must see love in everyone and everything. We must know without exception that God exists everywhere and within everyone and everything. When you view the world, see the face of God everywhere you look—even in your mortal enemy. We must also understand that everything in life is perfect as it is in this moment because we are, and all of life is the creation of the divine. Our lives are not an accident or a random spin at the roulette wheel. Everything happens and is happening for a reason. Trust that God has the perfect plan for you. Know that failure is only a mere redirection toward a better reality. Live in conscious awareness. If at the moment your reality seems far from perfect, then look to see and simply ask what message the universe is trying to give you. Ask yourself if there is a lesson for you to learn? If you are patient and open, the answers will come. I personally have come to realize that my life is just one big flashing signpost if I keep my eyes open long enough to see it. Most importantly, trust and surrender to the divine. We can't see what the future holds, so why would be want to paper the trial with limiting beliefs?

> There is an orderliness in the universe, there is an unalterable law governing everything and every being that exists or lives. It is no blind law; for no blind law can govern the conduct of living beings.
>
> —(Mahatma Gandhi, Nonviolent Political and Spiritual Leader of India)

Clumsy Means Something

As a strange example, if I find myself tripping a lot when I walk, I stop to do self-inquiry about what is going on in my life that is not smoothly "moving forward." I know that sounds odd, but as a rule, I am not clumsy. So tripping is a cue for me that I need to sit down and see where I need to pay attention and make some changes about how I am moving forward in my life. More often than not, I figure out the message. When I do, I stop tripping. But sometimes, I miss it altogether. Either way, I do heed the signs.

This teaching and understanding was strong in the Native American culture. They too believed that everything in nature was a sign, the animals, elements, etc. It was through this oneness with the earth that they survived some rather harsh conditions. This is often how they made their predictions about the future. So although it may sound a bit peculiar, the practice dates back a lot farther than I do.

A good depiction of heeding the signs of our lives was in the movie *Bruce Almighty*. In the movie there is a scene where Jim Carrey was angry with God, and he said, "God, if you're out there, show me a sign." He was driving in his car, ready to drive into a particularly bad situation. In front of him was a truck containing a number of road signs that said, "Stop, Do Not Enter," etc. God was giving him exactly what he was asking for in that moment. Clouded by frustration with the divine, he didn't pay attention to what was right in front of him and had an accident. This is a great example of understanding that you can't decide what your answer (or signs) will look like, how it will come, or who will deliver it. Just trust that the answers are coming, be open, and keep a watchful eye.

From There

The next step of love comes in the form of forgiveness. If you have people in your life that you have not forgiven, change that as soon as you can. If you aren't ready to forgive, figure out what is holding you back from releasing your negative emotions. Figure out how to break through and move forward. Harboring anger from the past is not the pathway to love. You can't truly love anyone until you have forgiven everyone, including yourself. Often times, we let go of resentment toward others, but can't seem to find a space in our hearts for ourselves. Nothing you've done is really wrong or bad. It is just part of the journey and sometimes needs to be recognized as nothing more than that. Learn from mistakes. Take them as opportunites to grow and develop, but don't continue to punish yourself for the past. It doesn't lend to securing a productive or healthy future. But more than that, you are worthy of all the love and light in the world. You are a beautiful, divine soul. Find a place in your heart for yourself and forgive all your past transgressions and move forward in love.

From there, you must develop an attitude of gratitude for everything around you, no matter how small. One of the best things you can do is to keep a gratitude journal. Every night before bed, write down anything that you are grateful for in your life. This will put you in a good space before you go to sleep. When you awake, read what you wrote the night before as this will start off your day on a positive foot.

If you are in the middle of a crisis, stop, breathe, and mentally take account for what is good in that moment. No matter how serious an issue may seem to be, there is *always* a positive point that you can extract from any situation. Working to focus on the good will move you through what you perceive as bad with less impact. Furthermore, when we keep an attitude of gratitude, we are less likely to be caught in the web of desires, which inevitably leads to despair, depression, anxiety, fear, and sadness for what we don't have in our lives. The happiness and peace comes when we are always reminding ourselves to stay acutely aware of what we have to do have.

Integrity

And last but not least, as I mentioned in the very beginning, you must have integrity—the alignment of your thoughts, words, and deeds. As a simple example, if you say that you are going to drink two liters of water today, make sure that you finish every drop. If you tell your friend you are going to meet them at 5:00 p.m., be there at 5:00 p.m. If you tell yourself that you are not going to quarrel with your partner, simply don't. I personally tend to find it very helpful to write out the things I want to complete each day on a list. It helps to see what we need to accomplish as opposed to trying to constantly jog our memories throughout the day. It also gives you a plan. You will have less of a chance of failure if you can see where you need to begin and end. As an added measure, I sign my name at the end of the daily or weekly list, as if I was contracting with myself to complete the tasks. Figure out a way that works for you and have the integrity to follow through with your strategy.

Granted, this is all easier said than done. But remember, with any change of habit, you need time, patience, and perseverance. Statistically, it tends to take twenty-one (although some say twenty-eight) days to change a habit. Keep that in mind, and be gentle with yourself. Nothing worthwhile comes easily, but positive change is easily worthwhile.

> The goal you set must be challenging. At the same time, it should be realistic and attainable, not impossible to reach. It should be challenging enough to make you stretch, but not so far that you break.
>
> —(Rick Hansen, Canadian Paralympian)

Getting Started

Start out with small achievable goals such as "Today I am going to smile at everyone. Today, I am going to spend more quality time with my children. Today I am not going to eat any candy. Today I am going to make sure that I hug my significant other at least three times." These are just some rudimentary examples. You have to decide for yourself where you need to start on the values journey. But remember, don't jump in over your head, or you will overwhelm yourself. Do something small each day that bring you joy and those around you. Doing too much at once leads to failure because you can't see your way through the overwhelming heap of personal and emotional debris. Change isn't a sprint. It is a steady run.

> You can search throughout the entire universe for someone who is more deserving of your love and affection than you are yourself, and that person is not to be found anywhere. You yourself, as much as anybody in the entire universe deserve your love and affection.
>
> —(Buddha, a sage on whose teaching Buddhism was founded)

From my own experience, from time to time, you may fall off the path. I do. No one is perfect; it is part of our humanness. But should you fall off the path, swiftly brush yourself off, quickly forgive yourself, and move forward, move forward, move forward. Know that at any given moment, you are doing the very best you can. If you could do better, you would do better. Change is a process, and it is certainly not an easy course to traverse. Awareness is a huge step on the journey. So understanding and seeing what you need to change is a tremendous first hurdle anyone can overcome. The path of change also takes constant practice. In fact, it takes 10,000 hours of repetition to master any skill. So, you have quite a lot of time to put in before you can make these significant changes really stick. Regardless, no matter what, remember, never give up as going back to the basics (our original nature) is one of the most important and meaningful things to be accomplished in this lifetime!

Tests, Tests, Tests

Keep in mind that once you start on this path, it will seem like the universe is constantly testing you to see where you are on the human values path. I personally have more than my fair share of life quizzes come my way on a daily basis. As an example of this, one particular week, I was really struggling with a coworker. We were just not on the same page about anything. It was a case of I said black, and she said white. The score was ego–3, human values–1. Try as I might, I could not seem to get a good handle on getting myself on track with her or my value structure. My ego was clearly in charge and not willing to relent without a significant fight.

Later that week (as I was abroad), I had to go to the US embassy to have some paperwork done. It was a complicated issue, so I was passed from person to person. Just as I walked away from the window where they finalized my process, I quickly came to the realization that they had forgotten to charge me. For just a second, I thought about just walking out. But then my truth and right conduct quickly overrode my false self, and I headed to the cashier window to sort out the fee. New score: ego–3, human values–2. And this is how it may work until you are living, breathing, and imbibing these values. Again, some days you will pass with flying colors, and other days you may struggle to keep yourself afloat. Don't get discouraged. Keep plugging along and remember to keep your heart open. It will all be well worth the efforts in the end. Charles Schulz once said, "Be yourself! No one can say you're doing it wrong." Remember that being a good person or a better version of yourself is not something that anyone can ever take from you.

In time and with practice, basic values will help and guide you through all aspects of your life. They are powerful tools that each of us have at our disposal at every minute of every day. These are our essence, the way, the beginning, the end, the road to positive change. They are everything, and they are the only real way forward for true personal fulfillment and positive societal and global changes.

> Life is the sum of all your choices.
>
> —(Albert Camus, French author and journalist)

It's a Simple Recipe

Life is really a very simply recipe. The best part is that you have all the ingredients you need to make changes within and around you to live it to its fullest. If you think about it, milk, sugar, flour, baking powder, and eggs aren't much by themselves. Mix them together, and you can make a delicious cake. So in life, metaphorically speaking, you have the choice to either just stare at all the ingredients (love, truth, peacc, right conduct, and nonviolence) and hope they mix themselves, or you can get out your utensils (love, will, strength, and courage) and get started on the process. The results of your efforts will be just as delicious!

Here is a small yet powerful quote to getting underway: remember to "start your day with love, fill your day with love, and end your day with love. This is the way to live" (Sathya Sai Baba). As I said once before, the practice is completely and totally up to you. The only magic in this prescription is to remember to keep yourself completely open and immersed in love. It will take time, patience, practice, and effort. You may even end up with a few emotional bumps and bruises as you are trying to clean up and weed through some of the excess baggage you've been hauling around or trying to store for posterity. But this is normal. You're a human being having a human experience. No one is expected to be perfect. In fact, perfection is an unobtainable goal. No matter how perfect you try to be there is someone or something that exceeds the flawlessness you desire. The idea doesn't exist as the notion of excellence is merely an abstract truth. Perfection is nothing more than a perception of one or a collective. The only perfection is unconditional love and the divinity you hold within.

Remember, if living the right way was easy, everyone would do it. Yet that is *not* the reality of our world. It takes determination and time to turn around our long-standing habits and then eventually the collective society. It is a process that is best approached one day at a time. As I have learned, sometimes it comes down to one minute at a time. But when you conquer that second, minute, hour, or day with your value structure intact, it cracks open your heart just a little wider until there is nothing left but love, goodness, and divinity. This is the goal. Divine, unconditional love is the ultimate prize. Challenge yourself to a higher standard. Remember, human values are not just a way to live. They are the only way to live!

> Genuine beginnings begin within us, even when they are brought to our attention by external opportunities.
>
> —(William Bridges, international author, speaker, and consultant)

What you say and what you do is your signature that tells the world about you. Go back to the basics, and make sure your signature says love, truth, peace, right conduct, and nonviolence. Imbibe good human values, walk your talk, and

W.A.T.C.H. Your

Words
Actions
Thoughts
Character
Heart (Sathya Sai Baba, Indian Guru, spiritual figure, and educator

Human values are not only the basis of a solid foundation, they are also the cornerstone of for building a strong moral fabic for our world. Ignoring our value structure or only tapping into it when it is convenient is not going to perpetuate lasting change for our personal growth or the development of society.

Everyone one has the capacity to be a better version of themselves. Everyone can give a little more, help a lot more, and take a whole lot less. We don't need to be a society that strives to have more, we need to be more.

Often times, people on the spiritual path seek to be enlightened. I know what that means by definition, but for a long time, I was unable to fully grasp what that would mean in practice. In truth, the concept never really appealed to me. However, I thought that was what I had to strive for since it was tauted as being the grand prize for walking the "spiritual path." Now, as I have come to understand human values, I have no other goal than to be, speak, radiate, and show pure, unconditional love. That's it. To me, this would be the ultimate reward for my efforts in this lifetime. But that should not be a goal that is not just set for me, the spiritual aspirant, a guru, or someone divine. It should be the focus of every person on this planet. Love is a seed that has the strength to cultivate, grow, thrive, overcome and forgive. It has the power to heal the heart and and save the soul. It is the core of our values and it is what will ultimately change the world one heart at a time. In the book, *Living in the Presence of God*, it states, "The limits of love are the limits you place on it." Keep your heart and mind open to the unlimited possibilities.

No matter what your position in life, practice, religion, or quest…remember to keep basic human values set as your guide and love as the compass directing your life.

> "Faith must become your walking stick, and truth must become your eyeglasses. Silence must be your mother tongue, peace your attitude, and love the very nature of your being. Righteousness must be your path and service your companion."
>
> —(Dewan 2003)

Helpful Resources

1. Guided Light Meditation
http://www.saibabaofindia.com/meditation.html
http://www.youtube.com/watch?v=Xi6XawC2SU8
http://www.saibabaforbeginners.com/light.html
http://www.saibaba.ws/teachings/jyotimeditation.htm

2. The Art of Living: Kriya Yoga
This is a powerful breathing technique that relieves stress and anxiety and produces an overall sense of health and well-being.
www.theartofliving.org

3. The Adventures of Meg
A series of books for children between the ages of 6-11 years of age. These books teach human values (love, truth, peace, right conduct, and nonviolence) in a fun, light-hearted manner that all children can relate to. The books also come with help tips and discussion questions for parents, teachers, and caregivers to further discuss each topic.

www.megsfriends.com

Order for iPad or Android: www.interactivetouchbooks.com

4. L.I.A. (Love in Action) and the Magic Backpack

A series of books for children under the age of 5 years old. These books teach human values (love, truth, peace, right conduct, and nonviolence) in a fun, lighthearted manner that young children can relate to. The books also come with help tips and discussion questions for parents, teachers, and caregivers to further discuss each topic.

5. The Center for Nonviolent Communication (CFNVC)

This is an organization that teaches the art of nonviolent communication.

www.cfnvc.org

6. Karen Drucker

A New Thought artist, musician, vocalist

www.karendrucker.com

Reference List

Brice, Makini. 2012. "Chicago Murder Rate Worse than Afghanistan War Zone."
http://www.newjerseynewsroom.com/nation/chicago-murder-rate-worse-than-afghanistan-war-zone

Dewan, Seema. 2003. "Living in the Presence of God:" Volume I

Gershoff, Elizabeth Thompson. 2002. "Corporal Punishment by Parents and Associated Child Behaviors and Experiences: A Meta-Analytic and Theoretical Review. *Psychological Bulletin* 128 (4). doi: 10.1037//0033-2909.128.4.539

Huffington Post. 2012. "Love ad Health: Research Examines Love's Impact On Us."
http://www.huffingtonpost.com/2012/01/31/love-health-stress-impact_n_1242349.html?ref=healthy-living.

Llyod, Robin. 2006. "Why We Lie."

http://www.livescience.com/772-lie.html.

Mayo Clinic Staff. "Forgiveness: Letting go of grudges and bitterness."
http://www.mayoclinic.org/forgiveness/ART-20047692.

McKeever, Joe. 2011. "Love Stories."
http://blog.nola.com/faith/2011/04/love_stories.html.

Pr Newswire. (2007). "Public Spending Up to US$10 Billion Per Year on Cosmetic Procedures that can Lead to Less Than Flattering Results & May Even Require Corrective Surgery."
http://en.prnasia.com/pr/2011/11/07/110322612.shtml.

Psychpage. "Relationship Reasons For Divorce"
http://www.psychpage.com/family/mod_couples_thx/divorce.html

Sai Baba. 2001. Sanathana Sarathi. August 2001. Prashanti Nilayam, India: Sri Sathya Sai Books & Publications Trust.

Shead, Mark. 2008. "How Much Time Do You Actually Have." Productivity 501. (May).
http://www.productivity501.com/how-much-time-do-you-actually-have/38/

Surakka, V., and J. K. Hietanen. 1998. "Facial and Emotional Reactions to Duchenne and Non-Duchenne Smiles." International Journal of Psychophysiology 29: 23–33.

Thenazereneway.com. "Meat and the Environment." http://www.thenazareneway.com/vegetarian/meat_and_the_environment.htm.

The Nizcor Project. "Hitler as He Knows Himself." http://www.nizkor.org/hweb/people/h/hitler-adolf/oss-papers/text/oss-profile-04-05.html.

University of North Carolina School of Medicine. 2010. "Corporal Punishment of Children Remains Common Worldwide, Studies Find." ScienceDaily. http://www.sciencedaily.com/releases/2010/08/100809111232.htm.

Women's Health Magazine. December 2012. "Pants on Fire!" P.32

Woods, Patti. 2012. "SNAP:" Making the most of first impressions, body language, and charisma

www.sixwise.com. "How Hugs are Proven to Help Your Health: Have You Been Hugged Today?" http://www.sixwise.com/newsletters/06/07/26/how_hugs_are_proven_to_help_your_health_have_you_been_hugged_today.htm

Zhivotovskaya, Emiliya. September 27, 2008 http://positivepsychologynews.com/news/emiliya-zhivotovskaya/200809271036

http://www.divorceguide.com/usa/divorce-information/divorce-statistics-in-the-usa.html